UNLOCK
6-FIGURE
STRATEGIES
IN TODAY'S ECONOMY

MINDSET, METHODS AND MASTERY:
ESSENTIAL STRATEGIES FOR THRIVING
IN NETWORK MARKETING

UNLOCK 6-FIGURE STRATEGIES IN TODAY'S ECONOMY

MINDSET, METHODS AND MASTERY: ESSENTIAL STRATEGIES FOR THRIVING IN NETWORK MARKETING

TGON Publishing

TGON Publishing

ISBN: 979-8-9863774-9-0

CONTENTS

INTRODUCTION

This isn't just another book; it's a meeting of minds, a gathering of leaders, each a leader in the world of network marketing. They've seen it all, from ground-floor beginnings to massive successes, and they're here to share the map that led them there.

Imagine a convention in a book where each voice brings a different pitch; each story has a unique perspective on what it takes to be successful. These authors aren't just writers; they're legends who have walked the walk, leading teams to peaks they never thought reachable. They are the few who have the grit to turn adversity into advantage and the openness to turn their deepest challenges into successes.

Within these pages lies a diversity of experiences as vast as the industry itself. Books like these offer what no single great speaker or trainer can—a chance to hear from a multitude of perspectives, a range of voices, each with its own tactics, and a collective wisdom that will excite you to take more deliberate action on your business.

Every chapter is potent, every page a potential game-changer, but among them, you`ll find that certain ones resonate with you as if they were written with your journey in mind. Those are the chapters to return to, the ones to absorb deeply and study meticulously. They're the ones that will become part of your arsenal, the tools you wield as you carve your own path to success.

So, I challenge you — not just to read but to engage with these chapters. Approach this book as you would a training session with these leading figures. Pay attention to the lessons that strike a chord, and implement the tactics that feel right for your path. This is your invitation to learn from the best, to pick and choose the strategies that align with your vision, and to transform knowledge into action.

Let's embark on this journey together, flipping through a convention in a book, and find those voices that are not just speaking but speaking directly to you. Get ready to dive in, to connect, and to grow. The leaders are assembled; the strategies are set.

Rob Sperry

"Can't died when could was born."

— Anita Aschenbrenner

MIKE GOSTOLA & CARLA SHAW

- At the top 1% of their network marketing company.

- Have trained thousands on how to leverage the power of TikTok for automatic leads and sales with their industry-leading course RockTheTok Academy for Network Marketers.

- Mentors in the Attraction Marketing community.

- International speakers.

- 25 years combined experience in business and marketing.

From Traditional to Trendsetting: How & When To Embrace New Platforms In Network Marketing

Ever had something completely unexpected pop up in your newsfeed, yanking you out of your scrolling trance? Picture this: a laid-back squirrel lounging on the grass, leisurely indulging in a slice of pizza, its tiny fingers delicately wrapped around either side of the triangular treat. I couldn't help but watch and my imagination started to run...

Coach's Notes: Pay attention! In this analogy, the pizza-eating squirrel is a perfect representation of how unexpected opportunities can arise in network marketing. It's a reminder that being adaptable can lead to discovering unique strategies that set you apart. Always keep an eye out for your 'pizza moment' in the market.

Thin or thick crust? Does he pick off the pineapple? I started to wonder, is this common? Pizza-eating squirrels? Turns out, Pizza Squirrel isn't one in a million. Google claims there are nearly a million others like him and there are over 1,700 Instagram photos tagged #PizzaSquirrel.

Although squirrels mostly eat nuts and seeds (as we know). Google says they are opportunistic omnivores...Pizza Squirrel stuck with me long after I scrolled past him. Oddly enough, I started seeing him as a sort of mascot for network marketing. (You knew I'd loop this back to you eventually, right?)

Every day, my newsfeed bombards me with color-block posts claiming the latest and greatest prospecting method. Open my inbox, and there are DMs about them too. It's a constant battle between traditional approaches and new-age digital overload.

Coach's Notes: The shift from traditional methods to embracing platforms like TikTok illustrates the power of innovation in reaching new audiences. This transition is crucial for staying relevant in today's rapidly changing digital landscape. Embrace change, experiment with new ideas, and find what resonates with your audience. I had the opportunity to meet both Carla and Mike in person at one of my leader of leaders mastermind events. They are always learning the most cutting edge strategies.

While it's true that some things will never change...other things come and go faster than you can say "*Clubhouse*" or "*Threads*". It can be really frustrating to know if you should deviate from the proven or even add another method to it to see if you can get better results with something else...I mean... squirrels gather nuts but then there's pizza?

That leaves us asking the million-dollar question...How do you know if you should test something new? How do you experiment without jeopardizing what's tried-and-true? How can you feed a squirrel both nuts AND pizza? Here's the good news: You can, and we've uncovered a formula to help you know when to test something new or keep the blinders on.

Coach's Notes: Adapting to new trends is not just about keeping up with the competition; it's about leading the way in network marketing. The courage to try new methods can transform your business and inspire others. Remember, every big success starts with the willingness to make a small shift.

Before we deep dive into the formula, you might be wondering, who is this person rambling about network marketing and #pizzasquirrel?

I'm Carla and my husband Mike and I started accidentally in network marketing over ten years ago... because he thought I was shrinking his shirts. Of course, I wasn't shrinking his shirts. After he realized that, he stumbled upon a weight loss product on Facebook, that just happened to be from a network marketing company.

He ordered it and lost over forty pounds. Everyone saw how great he looked and wanted it, so we hooked them up. We had a business...

Except at that time, we didn't want the business. It felt like our upline had us on speed dial...He kept asking us about how many people we had left on our list (what list?!?). What were our goals (what goals!?!)? He wanted us to meet the 'leaders' (what leaders?!?). He asked if a leader could fly to our house for a meeting. We were getting certificates in the mail. I'd toss them out. This guy was super annoying.

So what did Mike do? He told him not so nicely "You feel like a cult, I'm not interested, stop calling me." We had way too much on the go. Mike was running a custom cabinet shop and I had a full-time career in marketing on top of raising two little kids. Maybe you can relate? But, in all that... Mike did pick up on the part about residual income.

As you may know, owning a brick-and-mortar business is an epic roller-coaster ride. We were paying staff first and some months had little left for us. After a couple of years of doing this... That's when Mike, (gulp), swallowed his words and called the guy back. "We're in. Teach us." It was at that moment we started to SUCK at network marketing. I mean it got really bad. We ran out of our 'friends and family.' We talked to everyone and anyone. We sent cold messages and trolled groups for our type of people. We'd post links to our products in groups and under people's posts. You never know, right?!? We did the hotel and restaurant party thing, and our business wasn't growing, it was shrinking!

Then our upline decided to leave. At that time, I'd had enough. I bowed out. Mike saw the vision and followed them to a new company. He went back to our list of 100. Enrolled everyone again, this time in a high ticket offer. Then that company turned out to be a scam. It was devastating. But, Mike is so stubborn and he still sees the vision. Sadly, the last venture decimated our warm market. So how do you start over after all that?

Mike thought there still had to be a way. Maybe we just needed a different way to build (back to the squirrel, maybe we were too heavy on the nuts? Should we try pizza?) You'll never guess where he found it...in Vegas!

Mike signed up for an event there to learn about Attraction Marketing (I came because I'd never been to Vegas). Who we met and what we learned at that event sparked a new light and energy.

So we went all in and invested in the highest level of mentorship to learn the craft. We also found a mentor in another company who was using Attraction Marketing in his business with great success. So there we were, in another company...and we invested $20K (split between credit cards) in training to learn something new. Fast forward a year, and we were barely covering our auto-ship. We were fighting, and missing even more time with our kids. It was embarrassing. We felt like we'd failed. When someone said "Are you making any money in that network marketing thing yet?", We'd want to melt into a giant puddle on the ground. Something had to change, but what?!?

First, we had to get REAL with ourselves. We knew that the answer wasn't to get more training, it was in us. We had to take radical responsibility for where we were in our business. We were making decisions out of fear and our belief was so far gone.Whatever we saw, we jumped into it because we had no idea how to stop and evaluate things. No checklist, no formula.

As a result, we chose a company that we weren't passionate about at all because we wanted coaching from the upline. We were beyond burnt out and needed to pause. So we took a step back from network marketing and started to focus on the affiliate side of our business. With consistent effort and investment, we crushed it! We were on the top of the leaderboard for months and consistently made enough to have Mike leave his brick-and-mortar business.

Through all this Mike *still* saw the vision in network marketing. This time he decided that if I go back in, I'm going to interview leaders and pick the best fit from leadership and company. After several months, he found it! The company, the leadership, and the team that supported our pioneering (#pizzasquirrel) spirit. WooHoo! What happened next is interesting. Our upline had systems built on Facebook, we leveraged them. It is because of that, our team was consistently growing. But we kept thinking what if there was more we could do?

We had experience running Facebook ads for affiliate marketing and we loved how with ads you could reach so many targeted people en mass and attract them to us! But we knew that wasn't duplicatable. There's a pretty steep learning curve and costs to run the ads can be considerable.

Fast forward a few months and OG of Attraction Marketing - Ferny Ceballos (who we've been personally mentored by) shared a training he had done called "How TikTok Works, A New Ground Floor Opportunity".

Ferny is a MIT-educated aerospace engineer. He is NOT known for his dancing, lip-syncing, or blue hair... but he is known for making 8-figures online! So we listened up. We were really intrigued. Could this be the free version of Facebook ads that we were looking for? Could it give our team and business an extra boost?!?

That same week we got a DM from a member of our downline... Bryan Akers, school teacher, Dad of 3, and the NICEST man you'll ever meet. "Guys, you'll never guess what I'm doing and how well it's working!" He was getting HUUUUGE engagement, millions of views and thousands of comments all from TikTok.

By now, we've learned a lot about what not to do, what to ignore, and when to take a risk. So we ran it through our checklist (aka formula – *we're gonna share it soon*) and yep, it was true, it had all the ingredients that made it worth testing.

Here's a few interesting facts about TikTok you may find surprising:

- Teens are no longer the fastest-growing audience; adults are! 30+ million US TikTok users are over the age of 35.

- High user engagement: Users spend an average of 89 minutes per day vs Facebook at 33 minutes and Instagram at 29 minutes, 90% of users use the app daily and the average user opens it 19x per day!

- #TikTikMadeMeBuyIt: TikTok is the top app for consumer spending: 1 in 3 people buy something on TikTok.

- TikTok is the ultimate equalizer and literally, anyone has the opportunity to reach millions of people and attract a new audience — even if you have zero followers. TikTok with its super intuitive algorithm finds people for you. If your audience has gone stale and you have no new hot prospects TikTok will quickly change that.

- "I don't google anymore. I TikTok" - TikTok replaced Google as the top website visited in 2021.

- It's super fun and easy to create quick engaging content that keeps your audience coming back for more!

EXCEPT... our first impression of TikTok was so terrible that we made our daughter delete it and banned her from it. If we wanted to test it out, we knew we had to eat crow.

Mike went over there with NO friends, family, or connections, 100% cold market. He was looking to see just how powerful the platform was, and to test if anyone with no influence could get traction.

First he got curious and studied how people put out content - what was performing well (e.g., getting comments, saves, shares etc.) along with what caught his attention and what didn't. This helped him determine how to create a TikTok (what ingredients to include).

He then took an attraction marketing approach - knowing exactly who he wanted to reach, what problem he was solving for them, their pain points and fears. He wanted to provide value and educate.

The big question he answered before creating was 'what do I want my target audience to know, feel and do?'

He also saw that polarizing content was performing really well (challenging common beliefs e.g., breakfast isn't the most important meal of the day) so he knew he needed to be striking a cord.

From our marketing training, he knew that powerful content had 3 parts:

1. Enticing intro (aka hook that earns attention)
2. Value (3 or fewer smaller concepts that educate)
3. What to do next (e.g., comment below)

What he didn't know was how incredibly powerful this format was on TikTok.

Now, even with this in his back pocket, his first few videos were kinda terrible and nothing was really happening.

However, he knew that starting anything new takes time and practice so he kept going, and he started to do three plus videos/day just to see what would happen.

Then it happened!!

His TikTok "You'll likely scroll past because I'm a man talking about mental health" got 1.5 million views.

A few days later, his TikTok "Things I used to think were part of normal life" got 31,100 views, and after that his TokTik "I left a 6 figure job to join the Mental Wellness Revolution" got 13,500 views!

In less than 30 days he generated 753 leads, 68 customers, & 109 applications to join our team.

Things grew so fast that we were struggling to keep up with the massive influx of prospects! (Good problem, right?) After three weeks of no sleep and sixteen hour days, we finally put a system in place to make sure all prospects were able to easily buy products and apply to join our team - on auto-pilot! From there we trained our team (#duplication).

Our results caught the attention of Ferny Ceballos, Co-Founder of Attraction Marketing and we became his go-to-trainer for TikTok. Two years later our team (from our leaders down) has brought in over 20,000 new customers from TikTok! We've even created product shortages from our viral videos.

People who struggled for years, earn more in a month than they had ever made online. People who never earned an incentive trip are earning them from TikTok enrollments!

We had so many DM's of people asking us how we did it, that we made a Facebook Group: TikTok Growth for Network Marketers and a course RockTheTok Academy with our partner Shannon Boyle (NWM coach, energy + mindset coach).

We could easily fill a chapter of this book with all the incredible results from TikTok. So yes, being a #pizzasquirrel can work, it can be business and life-changing. That's what brings us to the formula.

After being in the industry for over ten years, making some huge mistakes, and getting back up again. We can confidently say it's not just about following proven methods or taking wild risks.

The key is 80% of your time should be spent following proven methods (that's how you learn the craft), and 20% taking intelligent risks. The safe, tried-and-true methods deliver... and once you've dialed them in, they also buy time for you to test something new out.

This means that 80% is the stuff you need to keep your business running and duplicating, and the 20% is the stuff that (if it works) people will talk about. They'll find you to teach it to them. Now, maybe you're thinking, yes... There is another method of building I'd love to test. Perfect! Give yourself two minutes now and let's test out the formula.

Before you complete this checklist be sure to note your goal. Is your goal to expand reach, increase engagement, generate high-quality leads, improve productivity, etc.?

Question	Yes	No
Is your target audience on the platform (e.g., TikTok, YouTube, LinkedIn, Pinterest, Lemon8, etc.)?		
Does your target audience take action there (either share their contact info or buy)?		
Has anyone credible (from either inside the industry or in one similar) tested it and seen results?		
Will this either save me the cost (if there is one) in time (e.g., improves productivity) or will I make it up in sales? *Proceed with caution if there is a cost because in our experience, if there is one it won't duplicate en mass.*		
Will this count as an income-producing activity in my Daily Method of Operation?		
Can a 6th grader learn it?		
Can people take immediate action and see a result?		
Would this method take a few hours to train my team on? (*they don't need to master it, just need to be able to take action*)		
Is the method adaptable to market changes?		
Does the method comply with the regulations, and policies that your company has?		
Can it be seamlessly integrated with existing strategies and tools?		
Do I enjoy doing it? Can I advocate for it?		

8-12 yes' Test it!   5-7 yes' test with action.   <5 move on

There you have it! A checklist to see if you should have some pizza with your nuts. Before you run off to test your new thing...Go #pizzasquirrel!

We know your time is precious and we don't take it lightly that you choose to read our chapter today. We just wanted to say thank you and that we appreciate you! There is ONE last thing to keep top of mind; You are the CEO of your business and your LIFE. You get to decide how to chart your course and build YOUR business.

That means that at times people won't see your vision, they may look at you funny, question your decision and some may not support it. That does not mean YOU stop. You figure it out.

When Mike first went to TikTok he told our upline he was going. She said, "Go for it, you do you". At the time she had no interest but knew Mike's personality so she was supportive. However, if he waited for her to go there with him... we would not be where we are today.

So you've got a choice. A fork in the road, if you will. You can continue on the same path you've been following. (If that's working for you, great!)

If you're like most leaders and you know that the 80% is just the tip of the iceberg and you want more, you want even better, you want a 1-inch shift that could change the course of your business and life, it just might be time to eat a piece of pizza!

Go crush it!
Carla & Mike

"Success is not achieved through dwelling on or avoiding failures, but instead rising every time we fall and persisting with unwavering consistency until we stand as the conqueror of what we set out to achieve."

— Dana DeLorenzo

DANA DELORENZO

- Liver Transplant Survivor (2020).

- Division One Collegiate Soccer Player (shout out to Quinnipiac!).

- NASM and AAFA certified fitness trainer.

- First time network marketer.

- Top 0.49% of current company with downline of approximately 100.

Playing the Long Game, and Remaining Consistent Through Adversity and Downfalls

Finding Consistency in the Most Challenging Way

In 2019, I found myself grappling with the sudden onset of liver disease, a relentless challenge that gained momentum in the blink of an eye. By December of that horrific year, I received a grim prognosis; having just one month left to live with four young children at home and a life that still needed to be lived. Amidst the whirlwind of uncertainty, consistency became the only anchor in my fragile world, but it was a difficult concept to adopt given my situation.

Fast-forward to January 2020 – An angel donor lost his life in order to grant me the greatest gift a person could receive; LIFE. Miraculously, a life-saving transplant breathed renewed hope into my existence. However, the journey to recovery was no less grueling. Repeated cardiac arrests, collapsed lungs, and having been plunged into a month-long coma, I emerged back to life. While still intubated but coherent and facing the daunting tasks of having to learn to walk, talk and even eat real food again.

I suddenly found consistency to be my unwavering friend. The figurative saying, "one foot in front of the other" became literal to me. I didn't start my rehabilitation with a mile walk, but instead simply standing up from my bed on day one. I didn't feel as if I could push myself past that point; The thought was daunting. However, the thought of never playing sports with my kids again, or doing everyday things with them was suddenly even more daunting than pushing myself.

So, I began. Standing at the foot of the bed evolved into taking ten steps forward. Ten steps forward evolved into a lap around the hospital hallway. Finally, a lap around the hospital hallway quickly evolved over four years into becoming a personal trainer, whooping all four of my kids butts at every sport possible again, and getting into possibly the best shape of my life. The climb I had to make seemed so high, but with each small, consistent and deliberate step forward, I consistently got stronger and stronger in a physical and mental sense.

Though there were challenges appearing unconquerable, it was the relentless commitment to consistency that became my guiding light. Through the darkest moments, my consistency propelled me forward, literally one foot in front of the other. It is here that I found my resilience in the face of adversity in my health journey, but also in so many other aspects of life. It was in those trying times that I discovered the unbeatable strength found within the simple act of staying consistent – a force that ultimately triumphed over the odds and propelled me towards healing and a newfound appreciation for life and now, the permanent adaptation of the act of consistency.

Coach's Notes: Dana's remarkable journey is a testament to the incredible power of consistency. Her story vividly illustrates that our biggest challenges can become our greatest victories through the simple, yet profound, practice of taking one step at a time. Let this be a reminder to us all that consistency is not just about achieving success in the short term but about playing the long game, overcoming adversity, and emerging stronger on the other side. Dana's resilience and unwavering dedication to moving forward, no matter the obstacle, serve as a powerful inspiration for anyone navigating their own challenges, in network marketing or in life.

Network Marketing Found Me at the Most Opportune Time

Fast-forward to April of that very year. A good friend of mine mentioned her new venture and asked me if I wanted to join her in something that she believed was going to be life changing. I hap-hazardously jumped aboard the journey of network marketing without an idea of which direction to turn; a venture into the unknown for me. I had never been in this unfamiliar space before and it seemed impossible that I would ever succeed. This was all too similar to how I felt just a few months before; in an unfamiliar position, knowing I needed to rely on consistency to propel me forward.

Even with consistency, my beginning days were a bit rough. Today, reflecting on my initial presence on social media brings about a cringe-worthy realization of my past missteps, so as you can imagine I didn't start in the position of leadership; this came over two years later.

In this industry, the path to leadership and success encompasses highs and lows, victories and setbacks, moments of encouragement, and bouts of defeat. Navigating through this maze of challenges, especially in those early days, demanded not just newfound talent and skill that I never had to possess before, but an intense ability to stay consistent and dedicated to the unknown process. This is what separates those who thrive from those who succumb to misconceptions and eventually failure to continue in this industry.

Network marketing is ever changing so it is no wonder why success is not usually instantaneous. It is a journey of being deliberate, and requiring strategic thinking, resilience, and unwavering consistency. Picture it as the craziest roller coaster in the amusement park. The twists and turns are never ending, leaving even the most experienced entrepreneurs wrestling with discouragement more frequently than one might imagine. Yet, it is within these winding turns that a leader's resilience is forged. Climbing to the peaks of success, only to sink into the depths of challenges in the blink of an eye, is the difficult nature of this industry. It gets a person thinking that it is too hard, or it's pointless to try. Embracing these falls, knowing that each one brings an opportunity for exponential success is crucial to understand during these trying times, especially in the beginning.

Some of these falls may be harder than others. Acknowledge that not every day will be a triumph, and not every sales pitch will result in a sale. Embrace the setbacks as learning opportunities instead of failures and view the peaks as milestones on your journey. The ability to experience both successes and failures with calmness and tactfulness is a trait of a consistent and resilient entrepreneur.

Coach's Notes: Dana's step into network marketing and her journey through the highs and lows shows us the real value of keeping going even when it's tough. Her story shows us that winning in network marketing, like in life, comes from facing challenges straight on with consistency and not giving up. Dana's path reminds us that the real win in network marketing comes from sticking to it, learning from every tough spot, and getting back up stronger every time.

Overcoming Failures with Consistency

But, how does one maintain consistency in the face of such adversity and keep their tactfulness? Clarity of one's purpose is key. You must know your why in order to gain that consistency. Reminiscing back to my hospital days; I knew my why. My why was clear — to be able to continue being an incredible mother again for my children.

Why did you embark on this direct sales journey, and what fuels your passion? Whatever your purpose is, it becomes the needle on your business compass. During moments of doubt, you must reconnect with your purpose—remind yourself why you started, and let that very reason propel you forward. Keep coming back to it during your times of struggle to regain that resilience.

Resilience is a building block of our consistency. In network marketing, rejection is not just probable but sometimes necessary and guaranteed. The resounding 'no' is not a sign of failure, but instead a stepping stone toward success. I'm sure you have heard something along the lines of, "the more times you hear the word 'no' the closer you are to a 'yes'."

Not everyone will say yes to your product, service or opportunity. Embrace this, and redefine your definition of rejection. Reframe setbacks as opportunities to learn and grow. Habitual consistency and resilience will fortify you against challenges, transforming adversity into a mere ellipsis in your success story; it is the to be continued...

Time Management and How it Assists in Keeping Consistent

Time management is key to maintaining consistency. With numerous tasks and responsibilities competing for your attention, effective time management techniques can make all the difference in staying on track and maximizing productivity. By establishing specific, achievable objectives, you can prioritize your tasks and focus your energy on activities that will yield the greatest results.

One helpful time management strategy is to use alarms and timers to stay organized and on track throughout the day. Set reminders for important online meetings or tasks to ensure that nothing falls through the cracks. Additionally, consider using timers to allocate specific time blocks for different activities. For example, dedicate thirty minutes to responding to messages.

When in the hospital, I made sure my alarm was set for the big tasks and events throughout the day; mostly just waking up, and assuring I am sleeping on time to assure maximum healing. I mean, what else could a mostly immobile person do? I also employed the timer function on my phone. I would allow myself twenty minutes of time via phone with my kids prior to making myself get up to do my physical therapy.

I then learned to limit my time with a lot of activities throughout the day to avoid boredom, and to assure I kept my mind fresh and giving it a change of pace since I was stuck in one room all day for over a month. By breaking your day into manageable segments, you can stay focused and avoid becoming overwhelmed by the sheer volume of tasks. Mastering time management is vital for staying consistent and achieving success in this industry.

DMOs - Strategies for Staying Consistent for Long-Term Success

The impact of consistency is compounded– each act of consistency builds on top of itself. It's the daily, incremental actions that build success over time. The influence of consistency extends to personal development, which is an integral part to maintaining a successful business especially in this industry. We must continuously engage in our personal development, positive habits and daily methods of operation (DMO's), in order for business to grow. Embracing a consistent routine, whether in business, fitness, mindfulness, or education, amplifies the benefits of perseverance. You must develop habits that are aligned with your purpose and end goals. Consider incorporating daily rituals that align with your personal goals with your DMO's and let this be your guiding force.

DMOs play a crucial role in sustaining consistency. DMOs involve strategic planning and execution of specific tasks daily, weekly and even monthly, contributing to long-term success. Identifying and adhering to your DMOs ensures a fool proof approach, minimizing distractions, and optimizing productivity. Here are some of my non-negotiable personal DMOs, specifically pertaining to Facebook as an example, though they are forever evolving:

- Add five new friends.
- Comment on twenty posts from people who are not part of the company and are therefore prospects.
- Interact with twenty social media stories from people who are not part of the company. Make the reactions are well thought out conversation starters (ie. I love those heels! Where did you get them from?! I have to have those!)

(I call the above, "warming up my audience")

- Post something from one of my content pillars. A content pillar is a topic to focus on in your daily content that your audience will recognize as something that describes your lifestyle and beliefs. For example, motivation is one of my pillars, so each Monday I will post a cute selfie of myself with a motivational post, sometimes taken from a quote that resonates with me.

- After posting, allow the audience to then respond to the post and go back and respond to every single comment. Yes, every single comment. Doing so improves your algorithm and keeps your prospects in your feed and vice versa.

- Post five to ten stories (approximately 80% personal/funny/entertaining and 20% business related).

- Listen to or read ten to twenty minutes of personal development via books or podcasts each day.

Remember – these are just my basic non-negotiable DMOs, but they change from time to time and this is the minimum I allow myself to do daily. I do not spend more than two hours per day on these, and that is an overestimate.

Coach's Notes: Dana's journey highlights the power of sticking to your path, even when times get hard. Her story is a lesson for all of us in network marketing: Success comes from knowing why you started and keeping that reason close, especially when facing challenges. Dana shows that being consistent, managing your time well, and following a daily plan can turn tough situations into growth opportunities. Let her story inspire you to keep going, no matter what, and remember that your daily actions are the steps to your success. Your 'why' is your strength, and your routine is your roadmap to achieving your dreams.

Using Habit Stacking to Assist in Keeping Consistent

Repeated actions shape your mindset, and with practice become habitual. Consistency is not just a set of actions; it is a mindset that transforms challenges into automated building blocks. Nurture mental resilience and consistency by stacking the positive habits that you already possess with those that you are looking to add to your life, whether business related or personal.

Habit stacking is a powerful technique that involves linking new habits to existing ones to create a routine. By piggybacking on already existent behaviors, it becomes easier to integrate and maintain new desired habits. This enhances consistency overtime without having to over-think the planning of things, but instead to automate the positive habits you're seeking.

When I was hospitalized and woke up from my coma, there wasn't much I looked forward to. Being that my vocal chords were torn, I couldn't physically speak with my kids, but my family and friends visiting were able to Facetime them so they could at least talk to me. This was the one thing that I looked forward to the most every morning. I began to make a mental contract with myself; after someone called my children for me and I was able to hear from them for twenty minutes, I would be assisted out of the bed, and I would force myself to do my daily steps to get my muscle memory back and begin to walk again. I would then sit back in bed and do my daily breathing exercises to strengthen my vocal chords and respiratory system so I could talk and eat real food again. Knowing I would talk to my kids again later that night pushed me to get my nighttime physical therapy in as well.

Boom! This is where my habit stacking really began!

To use this in your business life, think of something you do daily that you genuinely enjoy and stack something after it that you might not want to do. "After I allow myself a delicious, hot cup of coffee, I will comment on ten prospects' posts." You can do this with several habits in order to make the act of consistency a simpler task.

Utilizing the Power of Teamwork for Consistency

Maintaining consistency can be challenging on your own at times. Thankfully, no one is ever alone in this industry. Surround yourself with a supportive network. Share experiences, seek advice, learn from other leaders, and offer support in return. Remember that saying, "Your vibe attracts your tribe." Rely on each other to remain consistent – become accountability partners.

By partnering with someone who shares your goals, you can leverage the power of teamwork to stay consistent and achieve your objectives. One effective strategy is to establish an accountability partnership where you and your partner regularly check in with each other to monitor progress and offer support. This mutual accountability fosters a sense of responsibility and motivation, making it harder to slip up or procrastinate.

To take it a step further you can incentivize consistency. Implement a consequence system with your accountability partner. For example, agree upon a consequence – such as paying a small fine – if either of you fails to meet a deadline or fail to remain consistent with given tasks. This adds an extra layer of motivation and consequences for not remaining consistent, making it more likely that you'll stick to your commitments. In the end, you'll either be really broke, or really consistent! No one wants to be broke.

Tying It All Together

Recognize the symbiotic relationship between consistency and adaptability. While consistency provides a stable foundation, adaptability allows you to pivot and evolve in response to changing circumstances in this industry. Merging consistency and adaptability equips you to navigate the unpredictable nature of direct sales with resilience and strategic expertise.

As you progress in your network marketing journey, fine-tune your consistency map. Regularly evaluate and elevate your goals and objectives, ensuring they align with your evolving vision and purpose. Consistency isn't about stubbornly adhering to a single approach but adapting your strategies in response to lessons learned and changing situations. Assess the effectiveness of your habits, routines, and daily modes of operation, refining them to optimize efficiency and effectiveness from time to time.

Start adopting specific strategies for mastering consistency. Explore time-management techniques, explore the benefits of habit stacking, and consider the impact of accountability partnerships. Tailor these strategies to suit your unique style and goals, creating a personalized guide map for consistent success.

Consider the impact of your consistent efforts in the larger picture of your legacy. How you navigate the challenges, celebrate victories, and impart wisdom to those who follow you can become a rewarding experience in itself. People are always watching leaders, and attempting to follow their footsteps. A consistent commitment to growth and resilience sets the stage for a lasting impact on both your immediate team and accountability partners as well as the broader network marketing community/those in other companies. Aspire to leave a legacy that inspires others to embrace consistency as the cornerstone of their success.

Network marketing is not a solitary endeavor; it's about building a community of like-minded individuals striving for success. Consistency is the glue that binds this community together. Actively contribute to the growth of your network, sharing insights, providing support, and celebrating the achievements of your peers. Consistency in fostering a positive and collaborative community amplifies the collective strength, making it an environment where everyone thrives.

Consistency doesn't imply rigidity; it can coexist with innovation and new ways of doing this. New consistencies can be added when practicing the same consistencies overtime. Explore how you can infuse creativity and innovation into your consistent approach. Experiment with new strategies, embrace emerging technologies, and stay attuned to evolving market trends. The synergy between consistency and innovation creates a dynamic force that propels you ahead, ensuring your methods remain relevant and effective.

By integrating all of these facets into your understanding of consistency within the network marketing realm, you not only expand the scope of your business story but also provide a comprehensive guide for new and existing team members seeking success as well. This emphasizes that consistency is not a one-dimensional concept, but it is a dynamic force that is part of every aspect of your professional and personal journey. Network marketing is a marathon, not a sprint. Quick success does not always last, and often has to do with luck – but remaining consistently committed to your goals, regardless of the challenges, is the secret sauce that distinguishes the thriving leaders in the industry from those who dabble and eventually fade out. Embrace consistency as your guiding principle, and let it pave the way for enduring triumphs in your direct sales journey.

DANA DELORENZO

"The magic you're looking for is in the work you're avoiding. Time to take action. It's your turn! Think Outside the Box, Show Up, Fail Forward, Stay Consistent, Smile BIG, Exude JOY, and Live A Life That Demands An Eternal Explanation!"

— Jessica Crate Oveson

JESSICA CRATE OVESON

- Won Longest Standing Incentive in Company History.

- Performance Advisory Board Member.

- Published Author.

- Grew a global team while competing for Team USA at 5 World Triathlon championships.

- Launched a new country while in labor! Established a sustainable business, supporting a work from home lifestyle and the blessing to embrace the role of a stay-at-home mom.

Cultivating a CHAMPION Mindset:
A Blueprint for Network Marketing Success

10 Keys to Win the Battle of the Mind, Unleash Your Talents, Attract Your Tribe, and Unlock the Spirit of a Champion

Picture this: A blank canvas awaiting the strokes of your ambition, where the colors you choose will define the masterpiece of your success. As you embark on this entrepreneurial venture, envision yourself as a champion. Champions aren't born; they are molded by resilience, tenacity, and an unwavering belief in their abilities. Your mindset is the compass guiding you through the challenges and triumphs that await. As a former world-class athlete turned lifestyle entrepreneur, I am excited to dissect the traits, strategies, and principles, together with you, that collectively form the blueprint of a champion in the dynamic landscape of network marketing. In the chapter that follows, we'll explore the traits that define a champion mindset, the strategies to overcome hurdles, and the principles that will elevate you from an entrepreneur to a true champion in the world of network marketing. Are you ready to embrace the mindset of a champion and turn your entrepreneurial aspirations into a resounding success? The canvas is yours; it's time to fill your canvas and create your legacy.

Imagine this: It was a cold and windy morning on April 18th, 2011, a day that would mark a pivotal moment in the life of a tenacious and resilient athlete. Stepping onto the starting line of the prestigious Boston Marathon, this tall, energetic blonde seemed destined to meet the qualification standard and advance to the Olympic trials. Every element of her preparation was meticulously executed—precise training, dialed-in nutrition, and a recent triumph in a half marathon. Brimming with confidence, she was well-rested, finely tuned, and ready to conquer the race. She toed the line with other elite runners from around the world all here to test their physical limitations and conquer their goals. As the marathon unfolded, she maintained a flawless pace, soaring through the miles until an unexpected misstep altered the course of her journey. A jolt surged through her body, and suddenly her left foot felt ablaze with pain. Undeterred, she fought to regain her stride, enduring each excruciating step with unyielding determination. Mile after mile, her body numbed as she watched her pace slow. Despite the agonizing discomfort searing throughout her body, she pressed on, conquering heartbreak hill and the remaining uphill stretch on a broken foot. The toll was evident as she crumpled across the finish line, finding herself in a medical tent. Faced with the harsh reality of a shattered foot, her dreams of making it to the Olympic trials came crumbling down, casting doubt on her running future. Faced with a defining moment, she confronted two choices: Surrender to despair or embrace an unwavering commitment to her passion. Choosing the latter, she embarked on a journey of exploration and resilience that would change the trajectory of her life forever. It would be this setback that thrust her into the world of network marketing. Backed by science with products aiding in an incredible comeback, her coach redesigned her training plan — initially daunting, yet soon becoming the foundation of a remarkable transformation. In the wake of cross-training, a newfound love for the strength and precision of her body emerged. Embracing an unforeseen opportunity in both athletics and entrepreneurship, she ventured into her first triathlon, a decision that proved fortuitous as she emerged victorious. Coupled with a zest for entrepreneurship, this marked the beginning of a remarkable journey that led to five world championships in triathlon as she surrounded herself with an inspiring team of wellness entrepreneurs. Racing from Lake Las Vegas to New Zealand, she proudly represented Team USA, while growing her new business, showcasing an indomitable spirit that transformed a setback into a triumph.

What hurdle is holding you back? How can you turn your mess into a message? What will you create? Who will you help? Where could your dreams take you? What connection will you make? What will you dare to care about? There are so many opportunities, so many chances to find beauty or to ease suffering... What if you said "YES"? What if that little girl will live a better life because you showed up, if that void will be filled because you cared enough to do something about it... if we actually recognize the opportunity that's in front of us, what are we to do about it? We'd have no choice but to change things for the better, to cultivate a champion mindset, to take our turn, go after our dreams, and truly make a difference. Let's dive in!

In the fast-paced world of network marketing, where dreams meet obstacles head-on, having a champion mindset is like rocket fuel for success. Whether you're aiming for the winner's circle or business triumphs, you need to think smart, and make bold moves. It's all about staying sharp and bouncing back when things get tough, whether you're hitting the track or the podium.

The runner's ability to push through physical exhaustion echoes the entrepreneur's capacity to overcome setbacks, learn from failures, and persist in the face of adversity. The Olympic journey and the entrepreneurial path share a common thread of unwavering determination, where setbacks are viewed as opportunities for growth, and challenges are met with a steadfast commitment to the ultimate goal. Join me as we unravel the intertwined narratives of athletic prowess and entrepreneurial spirit in this chapter, exploring the striking similarities that bind these two extraordinary pursuits. Through the lens of the track and the business arena, we delve into the heart of what it takes to reach the pinnacle of success, whether on the Olympic podium or in the competitive world of entrepreneurship.

Unhappy with my attempts to climb the corporate ladder and disillusioned by the pharmaceutical industry, with no hope of participating in the current Olympic Games, I took a leap of faith into the bustling world of network marketing. Armed with nothing but my experience as a world-class athlete, a dream to work from home while raising my own children, and a burning passion for wellness products, I ventured into the daunting unknown of the industry.

Becoming a champion has more to do with mindset than many think. Let's dive into my journey as we dissect the traits, strategies, and principles that collectively form the blueprint of a champion in the dynamic landscape of network marketing.

Coach's Notes: About 4 years ago I first met Jessica at a Sundance Mastermind I hosted. She is one of those infectious personalities that has so much positivity. In this chapter Jessica shows us how turning tough times into learning moments can lead us to win in network marketing. She switched from sports to business without missing a beat, using her go-getter spirit. Let's learn from her to spot chances for growth and to keep pushing, no matter what comes our way.

The Traits of a Champion Mindset

I: Seeds of Resilience

Champions bounce back from setbacks with an unwavering spirit. They view challenges not as roadblocks but as stepping stones toward growth. Embrace resilience as your anchor in the face of adversity.

In the early days of my network marketing journey, challenges were like unexpected storms, testing my resilience. One particular setback left me questioning the viability of the venture. Instead of succumbing to doubt, I decided to apply my athletic background and plant seeds of resilience. Each challenge became a new opportunity to learn and adapt. I started a resilience journal, documenting not only the obstacles faced but also the valuable lessons extracted. The journal became a chronicle of growth, a testament to the power of resilience in cultivating the champion mindset. With every setback, I bounced back, stronger and more determined.

Tip: Embrace challenges as opportunities for growth. Keep a journal to reflect on setbacks, extract lessons, and outline actionable steps to overcome them. Imagine the resilience journal as a garden where each challenge is a seed. Water them with reflection, nurture them with lessons, and watch them grow into the strong, resilient plants that define your journey. Resilience is not just about bouncing back; it's about learning and evolving.

II: The Visionary Canvas

A champion's mindset is grounded in a clear and compelling vision. Define your purpose, set tangible goals, and let your vision be the guiding light through the entrepreneurial labyrinth.

A mentor at the very early stages of my network marketing journey encouraged me to create a vision board; it was a detailed canvas painted with vivid strokes of purpose. Since as early as I could remember, my vision had always been laser-focused. As a competitive athlete, I would mentally prepare for races by envisioning the race unfolding successfully. This practice of visualizing success helped me stay motivated and perform at my best. In my entrepreneurship journey, I applied the same approach. My vision went beyond simply selling products. I wanted to build a legacy of transformation within a community of wellness enthusiasts. This vision encompassed the idea of making a positive impact on people's lives and creating a community that shared my passion for wellness. This clarity of purpose served as a compass through the labyrinth of uncertainties, setting the stage for the champion mindset to thrive.

Tip: Treat your vision as a living masterpiece; the roadmap to success. Define your vision with specificity. Outline short-term and long-term goals, making them measurable and achievable. The visionary canvas is almost never static; it continually evolves with the business. Regular revisits to this canvas allowed you to refine strategies and adjust sails in the ever-changing winds of entrepreneurship.

III: The Dance of Adaptability

In the ever-evolving landscape of network marketing, adaptability is non-negotiable. Champions thrive on change, staying agile and embracing innovation to stay ahead of the curve.

As the industry evolved, so did my approach; there was a constant dance of strategic evolution. Attending industry conferences and networking events became a form of rhythmic movement, keeping pace with the beats of change. The business strategy, like a choreographed routine, adjusted seamlessly to new trends. My adaptability became a distinguishing feature, ensuring that the entrepreneurial dance remained both dynamic and elegant. Adaptability, the third trait of a champion, became paramount over the course of my network marketing career. I learned to embrace change, introduce innovative strategies, and stay ahead of trends. The ability to pivot seamlessly in the face of evolving landscapes kept my entrepreneurial journey dynamic and rewarding.

Tip: Imagine your business strategy as a dance routine. Practice new steps, stay in tune with the rhythm of the market, and be ready to improvise when the music of industry trends changes. Stay informed about industry trends and emerging technologies. Network with peers and attend conferences to gain insights. Create a flexible business strategy that can adapt to changes swiftly. Adaptability is a strategic advantage in a dynamic market.

IV: Lessons in Continuous Learning

The pursuit of knowledge is a hallmark of champions. Stay curious, seek insights, and commit to lifelong learning. Your ability to evolve is directly proportional to your commitment to staying informed.

The pursuit of knowledge is a constant companion on a network marketer's journey. Like a champion athlete refining skills, I realized how important it was to engage in continuous learning. Attending workshops, reading industry insights, and seeking mentorship became routine. It wasn't just about acquiring information; it was about exploring the vast landscape of insights and wisdom. My thirst for knowledge propelled me daily toward mastery.

Tip: Picture yourself as an explorer on a quest for knowledge. Each book, webinar, or mentorship session is a new discovery that adds to your treasure trove of insights. Develop a habit of reading industry publications, books, and attending relevant webinars. Seek mentorship from experienced professionals. Allocate time each week for learning to stay ahead in your field. Knowledge is power. Your commitment to continuous learning will become a source of competitive advantage, ensuring relevance in an ever-evolving market.

V: Connections that Transcend Transactions: Empathy and Relationship Building

Networking is the heartbeat of network marketing. Cultivate genuine connections by practicing empathy. A champion understands the power of relationships, turning transactions into transformations.

Networking for me wasn't a robotic exchange of business cards; it was an art of connection forged with empathy and relationship building. One particular networking event led to a profound conversation with a fellow entrepreneur. By actively listening and understanding each other's goals, a genuine connection emerged. It wasn't just a transaction; it was the beginning of a collaborative journey towards success. These genuine connections forged transformed transactions into transformative experiences. I understood the power of authentic relationships, a hallmark of the champion mindset.

Tip: Envision networking as a gallery of relationships. Each connection is a unique piece of art. Practice active listening and empathy in your interactions. Build genuine connections by understanding the needs and aspirations of others. Nurture them with authenticity, and watch your gallery grow into a masterpiece of collaborative success.

Coach's Notes: In exploring resilience, vision, adaptability, continuous learning, and genuine connections, we're given a blueprint for achieving success in network marketing. These key traits are essential not just for overcoming personal hurdles but also for strategic business growth. Adopting these qualities will help you navigate the complex world of network marketing, turning every challenge into an opportunity for success.

VI: Overcoming Hurdles, One Solution at a Time

Cultivating a champion mindset involves resilience, adaptability, and a commitment to growth. It entails confronting difficulties with determination, extracting value from setbacks, and using each experience as a stepping stone toward success. Facing challenges head-on, I collaborated with my team and approached each one with mindful problem-solving skills. Each hurdle was dissected, strategies were devised, and solutions implemented. Adversity became a catalyst for innovation, and failure was reframed as valuable feedback.

Tip: View challenges as puzzles to solve. Prioritize them based on impact and urgency. Break them down into smaller pieces, seek input from your team or mentors, and piece together the solutions one step at a time. Solutions often emerge when problems are approached systematically.

VII: Growth Mindset Unleashed

Champions foster a growth mindset, recognizing that abilities can be developed. Embrace challenges as opportunities to expand your capabilities and evolve into a more formidable entrepreneur.

My journey of cultivating a growth mindset resembled an artist transforming a blank canvas. Instead of fixed limitations, every challenge was an opportunity to add new strokes to the canvas of capabilities. Surrounding myself with a community of like-minded individuals, I embraced the "yet" mentality. Each skill developed was a brushstroke, contributing to the masterpiece of a growth-oriented entrepreneur. The journey wasn't solely about achieving success; it was about continual self-improvement every day. The champion mindset flourished with the conviction that abilities could be cultivated and perfected.

Tip: Envision your growth journey as an ever-expanding canvas. Each challenge is an opportunity to paint a new skill or capability. Instead of saying, "I can't do this," say, "I can't do this, yet." View challenges as opportunities to develop new skills. Surround yourself with a growth-minded community that encourages learning and development. Embrace a "yet" mentality and watch your canvas evolve into a work of entrepreneurial art.

VIII: Authenticity and Servant Leadership

These are the principles of a true champion. Be genuine in your interactions. Authenticity builds trust, a cornerstone of lasting relationships. Champions lead with integrity, creating a reputation that resonates with authenticity. Elevate others as you ascend. A true champion in network marketing understands the power of servant leadership. Support and empower your team, fostering an environment where everyone can thrive.

In the realm of leadership, I wasn't a distant figure but a guide walking alongside my team. Leading by example, I fostered a culture of transparency and open communication. Team members felt heard and valued. Authenticity wasn't just a principle; it was a beacon that illuminated a path for the entire organization.

Tip: Picture leadership as a journey where you walk beside your team. Lead by example and foster a culture of transparency where every team member feels empowered to contribute. Encourage open communication within your team. Your authenticity sets the tone for the entire organization. People follow leaders they trust and respect.

IX: Consistency in Action

Consistency is the backbone of success. Champions understand that small, consistent actions compound over time. Establish routines and habits that align with your goals, driving sustained progress.

My routine became a daily symphony of actions, played consistently like the rhythmic beats of a drum. Daily habits aligned with goals, creating a cadence of progress. Small, deliberate actions compounded over time, leading to a harmonious melody that propelled the entrepreneurial venture forward. Habits aligned with goals, ensuring sustained progress.

Tip: Imagine your routine as a musical composition. Each action is a note contributing to the melody of your success. Establish daily or weekly routines that align with your goals. Break down larger tasks into smaller, actionable steps. Consistency is built through repetition, so make positive actions a regular part of your entrepreneurial routine and let your daily habits create a symphony of progress.

X: Celebrating Milestones

Acknowledge and celebrate your achievements, no matter how small. Champions recognize the importance of milestones, using them as fuel to propel toward larger goals.

Throughout my journey, the champion mindset wasn't a static trait but a dynamic force shaping every decision and action. From the seeds of resilience to the celebration of milestones, the story unfolded as a testament to the transformative power of embracing the mindset of a true champion in the world of network marketing. Amidst the challenges and triumphs, we paused to celebrate milestones. Each achievement, no matter how small, was a moment of reflection and celebration that fueled the journey. The celebration of successes became a ritual, while the milestone tracker became a scrapbook of victories, a visual reminder of the journey's progress. Team members joined in the celebration, infusing the entrepreneurial voyage with joy and motivation. As the story continues, so will the legacy of our team, my family and the entrepreneurial odyssey.

Tip: Envision milestones as landmarks on your entrepreneurial journey. Keep a milestone tracker to record achievements, both big and small. Document them, celebrate them, and share the joy with your team. Recognition of achievements fosters a positive and motivated work environment. The journey is not just about the destination; it's about savoring the milestones along the way.

In the field of network marketing, a champion mindset is not an exclusive trait but a cultivated state of being. It's the combination of resilience, vision, adaptability, continuous learning, empathy, and authentic leadership. Armed with mindful problem-solving, an embrace of adversity, and a commitment to growth, champions navigate hurdles with finesse.

Elevate yourself from entrepreneur to true champion by embodying principles of authenticity, servant leadership, consistent action, and the celebration of milestones. As you weave these traits, strategies, and principles into the fabric of your entrepreneurial journey, remember: The champion within you is not a destination but a perpetual journey of growth and triumph in the world of network marketing.

See you on the podium!

Coach's Notes: Embracing challenges, fostering growth, leading authentically, acting consistently, and celebrating every win are key traits for navigating the network marketing world successfully. This segment reminds us that each hurdle is an opportunity for innovation, and every small step is part of a larger journey toward success. Keep pushing forward with resilience and authenticity, and remember, the true mark of a champion in network marketing lies in the positive impact you create for yourself and those around you.

"Not everything that counts can be counted, and not everything that can be counted counts."

— Albert Einstein

ARIANA KANE

- Serial entrepreneur in the areas of health, wealth, sales and education.

- Been in the industry for 20 years.

- Made 6 figures her 2nd year in business and continued in the 100K+ club over the next 10+ years with that company.

- Founder of brands and events for Sales, Character and Leadership Development, Transform Retreats, and a Lifestyle brand that helps educate and fight against Human Trafficking.

- Currently a National Sales Director in Financial Services, a certified nutritionist and Integrative Life Coach with networking and social selling as the passionate 'side-hustle'.

'Priceless' Compensation: The Ways it Pays to Believe

Every once in a while marketing magic is made with an iconic, inspired idea, that when shared, hits a home-run and human hearts all at once. From that moment on, the memorable message, face, photo or phrase is forever bonded with both the brand and the people alike.

An epic example of this happened in 1997 when Mastercard came out with its new 'Priceless' advertising campaign, which has been referenced and paired together ever since. Its message was simple, powerful, loud and clear.

The commercials would begin with a voice stating the exact 'price' of all the things being purchased and planned in order to create a desired experience. It was quickly followed by scenes of friends, family and the *feelings* the experience had evoked, with the narrator coming in perfectly timed capturing the 'scene' and then the word '*Priceless*'. Without fail it brought a lump to my throat, tears to my eyes, and right on cue the voice would add the tragically terrific tagline '*There are some things money can't buy. For everything else, there's Mastercard.*'

Priceless.

In my short time with you, my hope is that my message lands with even a fraction of the impact those commercials had on me, by sharing the same simple truth, that the things that matter most, aren't things at all.

There's no question this industry is known for its impressive compensation potential, that can and *has* created life changing wealth for many, as I truly hope it does for you. But unlike the instant gratification drug we've become used to, that wealth creation can take some time.

So while you're working and waiting for your committed, consistent efforts to compound, I want to share some of the 'priceless' ways it pays along the way, that you might more readily recognize, care for and count the things that can't be counted.

The world and business of self-employed, side-hustling entrepreneurs and 'work-from-anywhere' dreamers, is not a perfect one. Nor are any. But what this model offers that most other traditional employments or corporate culture do not, is the 'What If?', the 'Why Not?' and above all else, the 'Possible'.

See, this path is not an easy one. Much like the yellow brick road there will be obstacles, wicked witches, fireballs and flying monkeys. But dreamers don't need *easy*. We only need 'possible'. But *possible* always needs *faith*. This is the 'why' behind the 'what', the 'brains' the Scarecrow sought, the 'heart' the Tinman hungered, the 'courage' the Lion craved and the 'no place like home' Dorothy dreamed of.

It is the faith fueled *BELIEF* that the road was worth it. That it could get them there. That they, and hence you can change your circumstance, your lot and your life, if you would but *BELIEVE*.

I promise it pays. In '*priceless*' ways.

I'm sure it pays in *countless* ways as well, but for the sake of our time together and to pack the most 'priceless' punch, I'd like to share four of my favourites with you.

Coach's Notes: This piece captures the essence of what makes some marketing messages unforgettable and deeply impactful. It emphasizes that the most meaningful aspects of life extend beyond material possessions, resonating with the core values of network marketing. Remember, as you build your business, focus on creating genuine connections and experiences that matter. The true wealth of this industry isn't just in the financial rewards but in the 'priceless' moments of growth, community, and the realization of what's truly possible when you believe in your path.

No.1- HOPE

Hope is my favourite word and my daughter's middle name. I believe hope is magic, but if you prefer science, there's plenty of that too. Entire books on the 'Biology of Belief', the 'Science of Hope', the 'Expectation Effect' and the 'Happiness Advantage' to name but a few, are filled with research and data showcasing the power of possibility, the benefits of belief and how it doesn't just help a thing happen, but the seed that *makes* the thing happen. Though hope alone is not a strategy, it's the fuel behind the effort, the motivation to move, and the only source I know more powerful than the fear that would have you freeze.

I was first introduced to the world of networking and 'possible', years ago in the financial services industry. I got licensed in both insurance and investments and one night as I was doing an info-gathering for a family I'd come to love, it quickly became clear they were in pretty rough shape. They had a line of credit maxed out and credit cards dang close, totalling about $55,000 in unsecured debt and based on their net income, two kids, and long list of expenses, well...the financial 'plan' felt more like a 'puzzle'.

But what got me, more than their liabilities or lack of assets, were the *questions* the wife asked when the husband left to find me some papers. 'I know we're not paying you anything, so I'm curious as to how you get paid?' After explaining that I would get paid by whichever insurance or fund company I ended up placing business with she said, 'So you work on 100% commission? I don't know *how* you do that. How do you live not knowing exactly what you make each month?'

The whole drive home I thought about her questions. I thought about their predicament and all they were doing to try and get ahead, cut corners, and say 'no' to things, and yet there they were. I wondered why I didn't feel I could ask back the question I so desperately wanted to know and seemed so obvious to me. 'How do *you* live like that? *Knowing* the debt load, knowing the strain, knowing *exactly* what you make each month and knowing it's not enough?'

But she did know.

Their biggest problem that may have started as a lack of funds, became a lack of hope.

You could feel it. Hope feels like sunshine coming through the clouds. Like the blip on the monitor of a flatlined life, or the single candle lighting the dark. It's the smile in your eyes, the skip in your soul, the whistle while you work. Or simply the product experience you had that *made* you want to share. Or the comp plan you saw that dusted off your dreams. You can feel it.

But hope has an enemy. All the good guys do. Its name is *discouragement*, and its greatest power is *distortion*. It makes you believe you are so much further from success than you are. Luckily, hope tends to do its best work in the power of a *pivot*. Another favourite. Maybe it comes from my college basketball days, my love of the game and the pivot being essential to it, but more because of how essential it is to life. We *get* to pivot.

The most hope-filled part of a pivot is that unlike what discouragement would have you believe, it happens *right* where you *are*. No 'travelling' necessary. Not in some distant future, but right *now*. Not a change in destination, but only in *direction*. That change in direction is the thing that opens a path to possible, our eyes to a new lane, and our hearts to a new hope. From no way out, to a new way out. Right then. Right there.

'Priceless'.

For those of you like me, who live for a happy ending, I thought I'd let you know that I went back to see the family to discuss a few products and possible plan. But I knew the best 'product' I could offer them wasn't a product at all. We talked about the basics with some savings, a small term insurance policy and a debt repayment plan that felt more like a slow and painful death. So, I shared the *opportunity*, how it changed my life and how I *believed* it could change theirs. I asked if they were open to pivot. They were. Right then. Right there. Hope came home. Dorothy was right, there's no place like it.

No.2- HELP

Being a single mom with a heart that was hurt one too many times, I began to almost pride myself in 'doing it alone'. This was not a virtue, but a disguise. One day, a friend seeing me struggle more than was necessary gently said with a smile, 'We all need help Ariana, even a hand can't wash itself'.

The truth was powerful, as it always tends to be.

We weren't meant to do life alone in some cloak of stoicism or single-handedness. We were meant to *hold* hands, to ask for *help*, to learn from each other, love one another, commune, care, take turns and share.

There will be times in our lives where we'll need a helping hand and other times when we get to *be* the help. But rarely in the world of employment or corporate culture are you recognized, ranked, praised or actually paid to do it. Almost never is the manager, VP or CEO asking, 'What can we do to teach you all that you'd need to know to get to our position as fast as possible?' Too little do we see people pouring into others, eager to share every tip, trick or trade to help someone else win. But this model was made for it.

When I was a little girl, Cabbage Patch Kids were all the cult craze and I wanted one more than I wanted to breathe. Christmas was around the corner and my passionate prayers to get one were frequent and fierce. We lived in a place with a population of just over 12,000 people at the time and the only toy store around wasn't a toy store at all, but more like an 'aisle', in one of those small-town stores you see in movies that act as the grocer, pharmacy, hardware store, and post office all-in-one.

One day my mom took me along to the store, and with four younger siblings it was rare I was ever alone with her. When she was done doing whatever else needed doing, she walked me down the toy aisle and... *There. They. Were.* Two Cabbage Patch Kids, in cuteness overload, with their to die for yarn hair pigtails, and perfectly placed freckles. Next to them was another doll that was one of those real-life looking babies that sure, seemed great too, but was no Cabbage Patch Kid that was for dang sure. My mom then said, "I want your help to choose which one of these dolls you think your *sister* would like most for Christmas?' My *SISTER*?! My barely younger sister and I shared a room, and we did not exactly get along. The only thing *worse* that I could imagine than not getting a Cabbage Patch Kid for Christmas was if *she* did.

So, I pointed quickly and confidently to the life-like doll and said '*that one*.' My mother paused, a little surprised and suspicious and said 'Are you sure?' That's when *selling* started for me. I pointed out its features, benefits and accessories as excitedly as I could until she was sold. But any happiness I felt in the selling moment was fast fleeting. I then felt kinda sick. I knew what I had done.

Well Christmas came and like any young child I eagerly tore into one of my gifts and gasped. There staring back at me was the face of the life-like doll I had pointed to and *not* my request from God for a Cabbage Patch Kid. My racing thoughts were many and I quickly realized what had happened and what my Mom was *really* asking me that day. God didn't do this. It was all me. I wanted to burst into tears but couldn't. The shame of the truth of it all was too big for my little heart to expose.

Though the lesson was painful, it was also powerful and profound. *I could have got what I wanted if I had only helped someone else get what they want. This* my friends, is what social selling, direct sales, and networking, is all about. It recognizes, ranks, praises and pays to do just that. *Help another.*

When you begin, you'll be on the receiving end of this, and later you get to *give* it and go after whatever Cabbage Patch thing it is you want by helping them go after theirs.

Lastly, let me say this about 'help'. It almost always means '*together*'. My single-mom hurting heart has had me pretending to be a 'one-man-show', but I'm not alone in that either. Too many others are sitting in what feels like lost hopes and broken dreams, but still somehow know that 'every man for himself' doesn't feel as good or as true as 'together'. In a world filled with 'look at me' businesses and brands, here we get to build a '*come with me*' one. Dorothy did.

She *believed* she was going somewhere great, somewhere grand, a place where hope was the heartbeat and wishes came true. So in meeting and hearing the hopes of the others, she did what love would have her do, and made the invitation "Would you like to *come* with me?".

Not for her. But for *them.*

The real joy in her journey and in yours, will be who you get to meet and help along the way.

'Priceless'.

Coach's Notes: Help isn't just a word; it's a powerful strategy in network marketing. To grow, focus on lifting others, sharing knowledge, and working as a team. Start by asking how you can assist your team, and be genuine in your desire to see them succeed. This approach not only accelerates your progress but also enriches your journey with meaningful relationships and shared successes. Remember, the foundation of your network marketing success is built on the help you give and receive, embodying the spirit of 'together we achieve more'.

No. 3- A VEHICLE

I think we can agree that all things are not created equal. There are run down motels and Ritz-Carlton, Bic pens and Mont Blanc, Kraft dinner and Caviar, Pintos and Porches. They are not the same. The vehicle matters. You know it, and so did Mario Andretti.

Mario Andretti was named Driver of the Century by the Associated Press in 1999 and again by Racer magazine in the year 2000. But *Mario Andretti* himself wouldn't have known he was Mario Andretti until he found Ferrari. As a skilled new *up and comer*, he entered his first Formula One race in 1968 but only won his first F1 Grand Prix in 1971 when driving for Ferrari.

He went on to win 111 races in his five decades of racing, but I often think of the significance of the first with Ferrari. See Ferrari was *made* for a Mario and Mario made for it. He had the desire and fire in his belly and only needed the right time and vehicle to showcase on the outside what already lived within. With that win, he was no longer an 'up and comer'. He was a *Champion*, and Champions hold a new identity. One where they now *expect* to win. So they do.

But the opposite is also true. Another quote attributed to Einstein says 'Everybody is a genius. But if you judge a fish by its ability to climb a tree, it will live its whole life believing it is stupid.'

This hurts my heart. There are way too many fish *not* in water. Too many people have jobs and lives *not* in Ferraris, but golf carts, that despite effort or intention, control the speed in which they go, and the places they're allowed to drive. Soon they believe it's *them*.

This business can get you out of golf carts. It can give you everything you need if you'll give it everything you've got, and you don't need to *build* the Ferrari. This vehicle will do *all* of the mechanics and everything else it can, *all* so that *you* can do the one thing it can't. *Drive.*

Then the only question is 'where are you going?'

When Alice was lost in Wonderland and came to a fork in the road, she asked the Cheshire cat 'Which road should I take?' to which he replied 'That depends on where you're going.' Alice hesitated and said, 'I don't really know.' To which the cat wisely answers, 'Then it doesn't really matter.'

But it does matter. It matters a lot. Because the *speed* in which you drive, the *way* in which you drive, and the reasons behind *why* you drive, will have everything to do with the certainty of where you're going, and how badly you want to get there.

The 'sweet spot' in life happens when your try *hard* becomes *try easy*, when the road feels 'worth it', you can monetize *you* by sharing what you love, when your vision finds a vehicle and your dreams have something to drive.

'Priceless'.

No. 4- A VOICE

I first met the amazing Rob Sperry at an event I had created and planned in Banff, Canada, hoping if I did a generic training event in the epic Canadian Rockies, somehow I could persuade him and other Global Speakers to come. It worked.

The evening before the actual event I held a V.I.P night for the guest speakers and one of them, now a full time Network Marketer, had in her previous life, been a Lawyer, Crown prosecutor, and Undercover Drug *Enforcement* officer.

Another of the speakers had become a dear friend and came all the way from Manchester, UK to be with us, and before his success in business had been, well... let's just say more of a Drug *Lord* type of vibe.

Yet there they were, the two of them connecting in a corner, engaging in stories and rich conversation of past relatable shared experience, even if on the flip side of the story's coin.

The ex-drug enforcement Queen and the ex-Manchester Drug King in the *same* room, at the *same* event about to share the *same* stage, being seen and celebrated as *equals*. In what other world would this happen? What business or employer can you go to that doesn't care about your social status or story, history or hang-ups, politics or perception, education or lack thereof. A place, despite all the reasons the world says you can't... you get to be seen, to be heard, to be *welcome*, and to *win*.

I got emotional that night watching those two with such a beautiful example and reminder of the zero advantage, zero judgment, zero privilege, 'level playing field' platform that this opportunity provides.

You get to enter a new Dojo. One not interested in the colour of your belt, what you've done, or where you've been, but *very* interested in what you will do, where you're *going* and how they can *help* you get there.

'Priceless.'

In closing, let me say this... I think when Einstein said '*the things that can't be counted*' he knew there was no way to measure the things that *count*. No way to know the *heart* of a (wo)man, no way to measure the longing, the love, determination or drive of the human spirit. But just because Einstein knew it doesn't mean your friends, family, society or statistics do.

I read something years ago that had no author, but I wish I had written, because its truth is my own. '*Unless someone can look into the core of your heart and see the degree of your passions or look into the depth of your soul to see the extent of your will, then they have no business telling you what you can and cannot achieve. Because they may know the odds, but they do not know you.*'

My beautiful friends, you are not a statistic. And if you are reading this book, it means you know it too and have been chosen. Not by others, but by *yourself*. To run, to risk, to dream, to do, to drive, to believe, and to bring forth what is within you knowing your gifts weren't given to '*get*', but given for you to '*give*'. I know you can. I hope you will. When you're ready (or not) this 'priceless' ride is ready for you.

Coach's Notes: It was amazing to meet and speak at Ariana's event. I quickly learned she practices what she preaches. This last section showcases the transformative power of network marketing to give individuals from diverse backgrounds a voice and a platform for change. It's a testament to the industry's ability to level the playing field, where past labels or backgrounds don't define your future potential. Remember, your unique story and voice are invaluable assets in this journey. Embrace them as you build a community that values authenticity, inclusivity, and the belief in everyone's capacity to achieve greatness. Ariana's closing paragraphs should EMPOWER you of what's possible!

"Connection requires vulnerability and the courage to be authentic and genuine."

— Brené Brown

LOGANN REMINGTON

- Author, Podcast Host, and Blogger.
- Speaker, Trainer, and Company Leader.
- Grew social following by 3,000 in one Calendar Month.
- #2 Recruiter for Team Members.

Sharing Your Authentic Self Through Storytelling

To forge deep and meaningful connections with those divinely placed in your journey, embracing vulnerability and authenticity in sharing your story is crucial. Relatability, in my opinion, is the powerhouse behind exponential business growth. Indeed, mastering skills for online or face-to-face interactions is essential. However, without the ability to forge genuine connections, progress will stall. This insight comes from a place of love and personal experience, not criticism. Initially, the thought of sharing personal struggles and triumphs in the realm of networking filled me with dread. Yet, understanding why sharing these aspects of myself was pivotal became clear when considering the dynamics of trust and familiarity in transactions. Simply put, people are unlikely to invest in what you're offering if they feel no personal connection or trust towards you. Vulnerability fosters connection, which in turn, drives sales. Becoming relatable necessitates a willingness to openly share your true self. When you align with your divine purpose and present your genuine self to the world, the rewards are immeasurable. While technical skills are undoubtedly important, this book—and particularly this chapter—is designed to guide you in leveraging storytelling as a powerful tool for building connections. By intertwining vulnerability and authenticity, you'll learn to create a magnetic presence in the digital world, drawing others to you in a way that feels both natural and profound.

Everyone has a story. Have you ever heard one (or all) of these sayings: "Turn your mess into your message" or "Turn your test into your testimony" or even "Turn your trial into your triumph"? The point of those phrases is that everyone has a moment where they feel like the victim, but at the end of the day we also all have a moment of victory. Let your own story be the victory in your message. Struggling to identify your story?

Maybe you may have experienced these:

- A single mom that couldn't afford groceries
- Battled addiction and unable to pay bills
- Struggled with your weight
- Sexually or physically abused
- In a domestic relationship and needed a way out
- Living out of your car
- Living paycheck to paycheck

You've probably experienced one of these or something similar right? I thought so.

You are likely thinking, "How the heck does this have anything to do with my business Logann?"

STORIES SELL.

Your own personal story WILL SELL.

Don't believe me? Go look at any top leader in any company you know. Watch a live, scroll their page. I guarantee you that 99.9% of them start off sharing their story because it creates relatability and builds connection. Connection is the number one thing that will grow your business.

You can have all the skills in the world, but if you lack the ability to create and cultivate connection (or as one of my personal mentors Brian Fryer says) nurture, you lose.

Cultivate Your Story

Cultivating your story will require you to get very clear on what your story actually is. To do that I have put together some questions to help you dive deeper, and answered with my own personal story so that you can begin to cultivate yours.

What is something that has happened in your life that you overcame?
- *For me it was sexual abuse and alcoholism.*

Why do you think these things can be impactful or significant for someone else?
- *I know that a lot of others go through both of these things. I have overcome them both along with the healing that is needed to do that.*

What do you want to be known for?
- *I want to be known as someone that has overcome hardship, and shared her journey to help others along the way.*

What does that look like?
- *It means that I will share every day the hard things in order to help someone else know that they are not alone in either of those battles.*

How can you use your story to become relatable to others?
- *People often hide what they are ashamed of or feel they will be judged for. So if I speak and share my experiences, then hopefully others will do the same. Or they will reach out to me because they feel safe now, and RELATE to me.*

People tend to over complicate their story because we have been conditioned to believe that if we are not talking about our company or products, we are not creating sales. But that is a lie, and that method of marketing no longer stands. We are in 2024 people, and people want REAL connection. Your story helps you cultivate real and authentic connection.

Actionable Steps to Cultivate Your Story

1. **Reflect Deeply**: Start with the questions above. Journal your thoughts and feelings to uncover the core of your story.

2. **Embrace Vulnerability**: Open up about the challenges you've faced. This vulnerability is your strength and the bridge to genuine connections.

3. **Share with Intention**: Whether through writing, speaking, or social media, share your story with the purpose of uplifting and empowering others.

4. **Live Your Story**: Let your narrative be dynamic, allowing it to evolve with you. Your journey doesn't end with sharing; it grows and enriches with each new chapter of your life.

Coach's Notes: To make your personal story a powerful tool in network marketing, start by identifying the key moments that shaped you. Reflect on challenges you've overcome and how they've impacted you. Next, think about why these experiences matter to others and what you want your story to convey about you. Aim to share aspects of your journey that offer hope, showcase resilience, and demonstrate growth. Use your story to build connections by being open and relatable. Remember, sharing your story isn't just about opening up; it's about creating a space where others feel seen and understood. Action steps include journaling to refine your narrative, embracing vulnerability as a strength, sharing your story with purpose, and living your story authentically, allowing it to evolve and inspire others continuously.

Remember, your story is uniquely yours, but its echoes can touch the lives of many. It's about authenticity, growth, and connection. By boldly sharing your narrative, you not only pave the way for your own healing but also light the path for others to follow. As we navigate through this year and beyond, let's embrace the power of our stories to forge real, lasting connections in a world craving authenticity. Your story is not static; it's a living testament to your resilience and transformation. You are the main character, it's your time to shine.

Strategies for Sharing Your Story: Bridging Confidence and Connection

Once you've honed your narrative, the next pivotal step is sharing it. This process is as much about courage as it is about strategy. Here's how you can confidently bring your story to the world, making meaningful connections along the way.

Cultivating Confidence

Your journey begins with cultivating an unwavering belief in the value of your story. Understand that your experiences have the power to inspire, heal, and transform. You must stand firm in this conviction, even in the face of judgment or criticism. I've faced skepticism from family, distancing from friends, and a myriad of opinions on what should remain private. Yet, it's crucial to remember that embracing your uniqueness paves the way for extraordinary outcomes. Embrace this mindset; to achieve the extraordinary, one must dare to be different.

Actionable Steps to Build Confidence:

1. **Affirm Your Worth**: Daily affirmations can reinforce your confidence in your story and its impact. Remind yourself, "My story has the power to inspire change."

2. **Seek Support**: Surround yourself with a community or a mentor who uplifts you. Their encouragement can be a powerful counter to any negativity.

Strategizing Your Share

Crafting a strategy for sharing your story is akin to planning a journey. You might not leap into the deep end immediately but choose a path that gradually deepens.

Begin With Bite-Sized Shares:

Start small with snippets of your story. This approach eases you into sharing more openly and helps gauge your audience's response.

Mediums for Sharing:

- **Long-Form Text**: Ideal for those who find solace and expression through writing. Blogs or detailed social media posts can be powerful mediums.

- **Empowering Quotes**: Use striking quotes against vibrant backgrounds to capture attention and convey powerful messages succinctly.

- **Reels & Stories**: For those who thrive on speaking, short videos or Instagram stories offer a dynamic way to connect.

- **Live Videos & YouTube**: These platforms are excellent for building a deeper connection through direct engagement and storytelling.

Actionable Steps for Sharing Your Story:

1. **Choose Your Medium**: Select the platform(s) that resonate with you. Where does your voice feel strongest? Begin there.

2. **Plan Your Content**: Start with lighter, more general aspects of your story. Use these initial shares to build momentum.

3. **Engage Authentically**: Respond to comments, messages, and feedback. Authentic engagement fosters a deeper connection with your audience.

4. **Iterate and Expand**: As you grow more comfortable, gradually introduce more intricate details of your journey. Your confidence will grow with each share.

Sharing Formula for Beginners:

- Hook Your Audience: Begin with a compelling hook to grab attention. If you're unsure, revisit the "Storytelling Hooks" section for guidance.

- Focus on the Audience: Before diving into your story, highlight what the listener can gain. Shift the narrative from "I" to "you" to create a listener-centric experience.

Coach's Notes: Building the bridge between sharing your story and fostering connections requires both confidence and strategy. First, bolster your belief in the value of your narrative, knowing it has the power to inspire and connect. Implement daily affirmations to remind yourself of your story's impact and seek support from those who uplift you. When it comes to sharing, start with bite-sized pieces on platforms that suit your style, whether it's through writing, videos, or live interactions. Gradually share more as your confidence grows, engaging with your audience authentically to deepen connections. Remember, your story's power lies in its ability to resonate with others, so craft your shares with both heart and strategy, always aiming to leave your audience feeling inspired and seen.

Embrace the Process:

Remember, perfection is not the goal; connection is. Your first attempt at sharing may not capture everything, and that's perfectly okay. With each share, you'll refine your story and how you tell it. This journey is as much about your growth as it is about the impact you'll have on others.

By following these steps and embracing your unique journey, you're not just sharing a story; you're inviting others into a shared experience of growth, resilience, and connection.

- Remember to include details of your story
- Highlight the listener's potential takeaway
- End with a question to foster dialogue

Ending with a question promotes engagement by linking back to the initial hook, encouraging a two-way conversation and enhancing relatability. Here's how I've applied it in a storytelling post:

"Convinced you can't do it? Always saying you'll complete something only for a couple days later you dropped the ball?

That used to be me too. I think so many of us always feel this too, but I'm here to show you that anything is possible, you just have to believe you can.

Until a year and nine months ago I said no to drinking. I decided at that moment I was done with the back and forth in my life, the excuses, the pain I wasn't facing-for the first time I was ready to be so committed to something I held no other option in my mind...

Happy one year and nine months of sobriety to me.

But this post isn't about that. This post is about YOU.

This post is meant to encourage you to make a decision. Did you know that the number one reason for inconsistency is because you still have "other options" on the table?

It starts with a decision. And one from you. Not from the outside world, but from your heart.

And since that moment I've been able to make more decisions and fully commit to them. All because of one decision. It rippled into every area of my life. Rippled into when I say I'm going to do something, I do it.

The most beautiful part about all of this is the excitement knowing that the decision will lead to something beautiful. Whether you fall on your face or you soar across, the journey and who you become in that decision is the most important.

So my question for you… what decision are you lacking? What decision have you put off? What decision are you scared to make? What is it that you so desperately want but currently feel like you can't??"

See the flow?
Don't over complicate it. Just share your heart, and the real you.

What to do When you Start Atrracting People from your Story?

When your story begins to draw people in, consider this a prime opportunity for deeper engagement. Here's a structured approach to nurturing these newfound connections into loyal followers or customers:

1. **Initiate Personal Conversations**: Directly engage with those who show interest in your content. This personal touch can transform casual followers into committed fans.

   - For Short Form Engagers: Send a thank-you message to new followers who engaged with your reel. Ask what resonated with them about your content.

- For Post Commenters: Respond to their comments publicly, then follow up with a private message to delve deeper into their thoughts.
- For Live Video Viewers: Thank viewers personally and strike up a conversation about a topic discussed in the live session.

2. **Build Genuine Connections**: Move beyond superficial interactions. Your goal is to cultivate authentic relationships, not just accumulate likes or follows.

3. **Foster Community Through Engagement**: Regular interaction encourages a sense of community among your followers. Their engagement with your content can improve its visibility, thanks to social media algorithms.

4. **Encourage Conversational Exchanges**: Don't shy away from initiating discussions. The more you interact, the more likely you'll spark interest in your offerings or message.

5. **Leverage Authenticity for Deeper Relatability**: Share your journey and insights openly. Authenticity breeds vulnerability, which in turn fosters relatability, encouraging more meaningful conversations.

Remember, the essence of attracting and retaining interest lies in being genuine, relatable, and actively engaged with your community. This approach not only boosts your visibility but also lays the foundation for a loyal and supportive audience.

Coach's Notes: "Embracing the journey of sharing your story is a process of growth and connection, not seeking perfection. Logann's transformation into one of the top recruiters in her company exemplifies this perfectly. Through coaching and applying these principles, Logann showed that by starting with a commitment to sharing authentically and engaging deeply, you can significantly impact your audience and business. Her success underlines the importance of starting with a clear decision, being open about your challenges, and consistently engaging with your community. This not only cultivates genuine connections but also drives meaningful growth. Remember, it's about inviting others into your journey, showing them the possibilities within themselves, and encouraging them to take action towards their goals. Be patient, authentic, and interactive, and watch how your story can inspire change and foster a community of support around you."

Copywriting Skills and Hooks

Mastering storytelling and copywriting is crucial for engaging your audience effectively. Here are actionable steps to enhance your skills and ensure your message resonates:

1. **Focus on Your Audience**: Before you begin writing or recording, clearly define who you are speaking to. Understanding your audience's needs, desires, and challenges will guide your storytelling.

2. **Craft Your Message with the Audience in Mind**: Whether you're writing a post or scripting a reel, always tailor your message to address your audience's interests and how you can add value to their lives.

3. **Start with a Strong Hook**: Your opening sentence or scene is critical. It's the moment you either capture attention or lose it. Dedicate time to crafting compelling hooks that prompt your audience to engage further.

   - **Use Engaging Starters**: Consider these hook examples to begin your story compellingly:

     ○ "Imagine this..." followed by a relatable scenario.

- "How to..." by offering a solution to a common problem.

- "Mistakes I made that you don't have to..." sharing lessons learned.

- "WARNING:...." introducing a cautionary tale or advice.

- Use a provocative quote or a surprising statistic related to your topic.

- "How every [target audience] can [achieve a desired outcome]."

4. **Prioritize the Hook**: Spend significant time refining your hook or headline. It's the key to stopping the scroll and drawing your audience into your story. Experiment with different hooks to see what resonates best with your audience.

5. **Iterate and Test**: Don't be afraid to try different hooks and storytelling techniques. Use audience feedback and engagement metrics to refine your approach.

Remember, effective storytelling in copywriting is not just about sharing your message; it's about crafting it in a way that speaks directly to your audience, grabs their attention immediately, and keeps them engaged.

Embracing authenticity and vulnerability in your storytelling can significantly enhance your presence on social media, fostering connections and relatability with your audience. By mastering storytelling, you not only capture their hearts but also potentially their financial support. This approach has been the cornerstone of building my brand and business, attracting more people to my circle.

Storytelling isn't a path everyone will choose, as it demands the courage to share boldly and authentically. However, believing in the power of your story and its potential to impact your life financially, personally, and professionally is a journey worth embarking on.

Remember, your story is your "why," and without it, engagement and purchases are less likely.

Oprah Winfrey beautifully encapsulated the essence of storytelling when she said, "Vulnerability is being willing to express the truth no matter what, the truth of who you are, the essence at your core of what you are feeling in any given moment. It's being able to open your soul so that others can see their soul in yours."

"I believe that being successful means having a balance of success stories across the many areas of your life. You can't truly be considered successful in your business life if your home life is in shambles."

— Zig Ziglar

KEVIN MOORE

- 25+ years of network marketing experience.
- Started at corporate office (7 years 1998-2005).
- Traveled to 45+ countries in supporting others and building business together.
- Sustained 6 figure income for 15 consecutive years.

Unlocking the Power of Connection:
A Key to Business Success

Sambungan, Tsunagari, Conexión, Uhusiano... No matter what language we speak, "Connection" is a fundamental aspect of any successful business. Since 1999, I have traveled to forty countries building my business, and one thing remains clear no matter where I am, there is a requirement for connection. It is a primal need that resonates with all of humanity. Forget about "stranger danger" and embrace the power of human interaction.

In a world where constant digital connectivity seems to overshadow genuine connection, the question arises: How can we combat this? Though building connections may not be easy, it is undoubtedly simple. Let's explore the difference between easy and simple. If it were easy, success would be within everyone's grasp. But the simplicity lies in something as fundamental as sharing; starting with meaningful conversations.

Are you seizing every opportunity to share your story? Mastering the art of small talk can yield remarkable results. You don't have to be "that dreaded person" to forge new connections and share consistently. Nowadays, almost everyone has a side gig or hustle, and society is becoming increasingly more supportive of those with their own businesses. Amidst ever-changing social media, technology, and artificial intelligence, one thing remains the backbone of every network; the people and the relationships we build. We've all heard the saying, "Facts tell, stories sell." But can we engage in authentic conversations that foster genuine connections and, ultimately, sustainable conversions?

In network marketing, initiating effective conversations is key to building relationships and promoting products, services, or opportunities. I've learned this through my own journey, starting as a corporate employee in this industry and eventually transitioning full time to network marketing. I decided to chase my dreams and get on the "right side of the right industry". To have the opportunity to build my dreams rather than trading time for money by supporting someone else to build theirs. Application is far more challenging than information. It requires skill and expertise gained through experience. It's like riding a bike - you learn by falling down and getting back up.

From my experience, most representatives invest time in preparing their "message" but overlook the importance of being prepared in the "moment." Whether online or in person, what are you doing with the opportunities to connect?

Small talk is about revisiting the basics. They're called "tried and true" for a reason - they have stood the test of time. No need to overanalyze. Start by establishing a genuine connection with the person. Ask about their interests, hobbies, or experiences. Creating rapport makes the conversation more comfortable and enjoyable. Authenticity is valued, so be yourself and communicate sincerely. Avoid scripted, overly salesy language that may come across as insincere. Before diving into product discussions or business opportunities, offer value to the other person. Share helpful information, tips, or insights that align with their interests or needs. This positions you as a knowledgeable and resourceful individual. Seek out common interests or experiences shared between you and the other person. This fosters a sense of connection and understanding. When initiating online conversations, follow proper platform etiquette. Avoid spammy or unwanted messages. Instead, engage with their content, leave thoughtful comments, and let the conversation unfold naturally. Choose the right moment to connect. Respect the other person's schedule and preferences. Avoid reaching out during inconvenient times or bombarding them with messages.

Personal stories also hold tremendous power. Share your journey and experiences in network marketing, emphasizing the positive impact it has had on your life. This helps create a relatable and authentic connection. Remember, not every conversation will immediately result in a sale or sign-up, and that shouldn't be the main goal. Conversations lead to connections, and connections lead to conversions. Be patient and focus on building relationships. Consistent, positive interactions pave the way for long-term connections and potential business opportunities. The foundation for a successful network marketing business is built on relationships and trust. Prioritize building connections over immediate sales pitches. Remember, genuine connection breathes life into your interactions, while a pushy sales approach can be off-putting. In today's world, we often find ourselves disconnected from one another. Never in the history of time have people been more connected via technology, but less connected in manners of true relationships. But what if we told you that starting a simple conversation could lead to incredible connections?

Imagine standing in line at the grocery store or attending a social event. Instead of scrolling mindlessly on your phone, open up and talk to people around you. That's what this business is truly about - seeking genuine interactions. You never know unless you try. Sure, rejection might sting, but it's nothing personal. If someone rejects your message, they're not rejecting you as a person. Don't take it to heart. What really matters is seizing the moment when it presents itself.

To spark these meaningful conversations, I practice the methodology referred to by the acronym, F.O.R.M. Let's break it down.

Coach's Notes: Kevin, with over 25 years of experience, underscores the critical role of genuine connections in business success. To foster these connections, start by sharing your story and engaging in authentic conversations without the pressure of immediate sales. Remember, every interaction is an opportunity to learn and grow. Action steps include practicing small talk, being genuinely interested in others, and sharing experiences. Kevin's journey from corporate to top network marketing professional exemplifies the power of embracing every chance to connect, proving that relationships are the cornerstone of network marketing. Focus on building trust and rapport, and view each conversation as a step towards lasting connections, not just quick wins. Now here comes the good stuff from Kevin!

Family
Everyone loves to talk about their loved ones, whether they're kids or furry friends. It's an easy way to kick-start a conversation and find common ground.

Occupation
By asking people what they do for a living, you can learn so much about them. Are they passionate about their work, or do they yearn for something more? Every occupation reveals a story waiting to be told.

This business isn't boring. Be creative. Fun is part of the fundamentals. I remember one such example for using occupation to spur conversation. I had a good friend that when asked his current occupation would say he was "a repairman." The first time I heard his response, I shot him a side eyed glance of confusion. I knew he was involved in network marketing, but then he went on to say, "I repair people's broken dreams." Although not spoken, I could almost hear the, "Ta-da." Queue the high hat chime for the punchline. But...it was a conversation starter, repairing people's broken dreams. Every single time I shook my head, but every single time he started a conversation. He knew it was goofy, it was tongue in cheek, but he started a conversation. The beginning of connection was born.

Almost every time when I talk to somebody for the first time, I inquire, "what do you do for a living?" I listen because that's always a key indicator. I can always learn a lot about a person by what they do and how they feel about what they do. Because sometimes they'll be like, "Oh, don't ask. I'm living for the "weekends" or they make a statement on how they are underpaid or under-appreciated. Most people know they need something more, but do they know what it is, how to find it? There's always opportunities. Here's the other thing, after I listen to what they do for work, they'll say in return, "Well, what do you do for a living?" That is the golden question and an invitation for me to share.

Recreation
What do people do with their spare time? Their hobbies, interests, and adventures provide a window into their true selves. If you see someone with a hiking backpack, strike up a conversation about their next outdoor escapade. You would be amazed at how people's passions and your plan meet at all of the perfect crossroads.

Motivation
Discovering what motivates someone is like unlocking a hidden treasure. By asking open-ended questions that delve deeper than a simple yes or no, you'll learn their purpose and dreams. Genuine interest and active listening are the keys to building trust.

I am not looking to convert or close people with initial interactions, especially if I am in a public place or community event. I am looking to capture. First, their curiosity. Secondly, their contact information.

Never forget, our purpose is not to pressure or convince. Instead, we seek genuine interactions, engagement, and filtering. We are looking for those who are looking for us. And believe me, they're out there! No matter what the naysayers may say, this model has endured and will continue to do so. So what if some people don't see the value? There will always be someone waiting for what we have to offer.

"Some will, some won't, so what, someone's waiting" is just as true today as it ever has been.

Entrepreneur, it's not French for unemployed! Entrepreneurs, remember this: Connecting with the masses is the way to dine with the classes. Each conversation holds immense potential. So let go of assumptions, judgments, and stereotypes. You never know the value a person holds or the impact they can make. In a world of social separation, be the one who brings people together. Start the conversation that could change someone's life.

Coach's Notes: To effectively engage in conversations that build genuine connections, focus on F.O.R.M. (Family, Occupation, Recreation, Motivation). Start conversations by asking about their loved ones or pets, creating an immediate connection through common experiences. Dive into discussions about their work to understand their passion or desire for change, providing a natural segue into discussing your network marketing opportunity. Explore their hobbies and interests to discover shared passions, enhancing the personal connection.

Finally, uncover their motivations to identify their desires and how your opportunity can help fulfill them. Kevin's creative approach to discussing occupation exemplifies how to make conversations both meaningful and memorable. Remember, your goal is to listen actively, share authentically, and seek to understand their needs and aspirations. This method isn't about selling; it's about connecting on a human level and identifying those who are open to what you offer. Approach each interaction with curiosity, empathy, and the readiness to share your story when the moment arises.

Embarking on my journey as a business builder in this industry, I found myself in Jakarta, Indonesia, where the company I represented was opening a corporate office. Recognizing the immense potential of this opportunity, I knew I had to seize it while it was still within reach. I am a firm believer when you have the opportunity of a lifetime, you must act within the lifetime of that opportunity. Making a bold decision, I invested in a trip to Jakarta to meet with a carefully selected group of ten qualified prospects who had the power to make a significant impact if they were to join our team. Acknowledging that some of these prospects had varying levels of English proficiency, I made the strategic choice to hire a translator who could effectively convey our presentation in their native language, Bahasa Indonesian.

This additional investment was well worth it, as I believed that finding the right partner would ultimately be invaluable. Over the course of a week at the centrally located Ritz Carlton, I met with each individual for one-on-one sessions. However, to my dismay, each meeting ended in rejection. The timing wasn't right, circumstances didn't align, expectations weren't met - there seemed to be one reason after another why it wasn't the perfect fit. Feeling frustrated, defeated, and ultimately deflated, I sat down with my translator on the final day to express my gratitude for her exceptional work and settle the payment for her services. As we conversed in a lounge, our discussion touched upon the notion that sometimes, taking risks is necessary to achieve success, and that not every endeavor will yield positive results. During this conversation, I began to learn more about her. In time, she shared her struggles as a translator - how it was often difficult to secure clients and the work wasn't always fulfilling. While the compensation was decent when she did manage to find jobs, they were becoming increasingly scarce. It was in that moment that I truly saw the potential in front of me. The irony of the situation hit me - I had traveled across the world to recruit from a predetermined list of top candidates, yet the best prospect had been right beside me the entire time. The person who had been faithfully translating our presentations became the partner I never knew I had.

Our connection led her to fully believe in the message she had skillfully translated throughout the week. I almost missed out on this incredible opportunity because I had underestimated her potential. I had overlooked her. Thankfully, I realized my mistake in time and she ultimately joined our team, becoming a top-ranking leader and highly successful producer in the Indonesian market.

Another example is the courtship of my beautiful wife. It is truly the greatest prospecting story of my life. It goes to show that with determination and the courage to take on a challenge, you can achieve the seemingly impossible. From the moment I first met her, I knew I wanted to start my life's team with her, but it would be no small task. I refused to let fear hold me back. I pursued her relentlessly, putting in the effort to show her how much I cared, and it paid off. As my greatest source of strength and wisdom, she reminds me of a valuable lesson that has shaped my approach to everything: it's not about how much knowledge or expertise you have. It's about how much you genuinely care about others.

My wife's favorite quote, "People don't care how much you know until they know how much you care," has become my mantra. It's a reminder that building meaningful connections and showing empathy is what truly matters in any endeavor. So, if you ever find yourself faced with a daunting challenge or a vital correspondence, let her reminder ring true. Believe in yourself, overcome your fears, and let your genuine care for others be your guiding force. The results might just exceed your wildest expectations.

The key to forming meaningful connections is to shift our perspective away from ourselves and focus on the other person. We've all heard the saying, "God gave us two ears and one mouth and so listen twice as much as you speak," and it holds true for building strong bonds. I like to call this concept the "photograph philosophy." As a proud father of six, I've noticed something fascinating when I show my children a family photo. Their attention is immediately drawn to themselves, not out of vanity or narcissism, but because it's human nature to prioritize our own experiences. Dale Carnegie captured this truth perfectly when he said, "A person's name is the sweetest sound in any language."

So why do we often witness individuals in this industry approaching important conversations as if they're about to give a solo performance, warming up with a barrage of "me, me, me", solely focused on themselves? Shifting our mindset to prioritize the other person can be incredibly effective for creating meaningful connections. How do we polish that practice? How can small talk lead to big business?

Imagine a world where people are increasingly closed off, pessimistic, and sometimes cold. A world where disagreements are quickly divvied up and collaboration takes a backseat. Unfortunately, this is the reality we increasingly face today. But let me share something I've observed during my world travel; there are places where communities embrace newcomers with open arms, creating traditions of welcome and celebration. Unfortunately in America, our default mindset when buying a new house or building a home often revolves around marking our territory with fences. It may seem cynical, but it's a reality we can't ignore. Now, I'm not saying that putting up fences is a bad thing. In fact, there's a quote from Robert Frost that says "Good fences make good neighbors." But it's important to recognize the impact this mindset has on our interactions with others.

Society has trapped us in a rigid mindset, programming us to follow the status quo and believe that there is only one path to financial stability or professional achievement. Joseph Goebbels says "If you tell a lie loud enough and long enough, people will eventually come to believe it." But amidst all the falsehoods that manipulate our thinking, there is real hope. The American dream may appear dormant for some, but it is still very much alive in the hearts and minds of many. You can witness it when you ask someone about their childhood dreams; the answer is ready to burst out, eagerly waiting to be realized.

In our quest to embrace meaningful encounters, one crucial skill we must master is the art of authentic acknowledgment. It begins by recognizing others as individuals, equals, and more than mere statistics on a spreadsheet, points towards an incentive trip, or a future bonus to be paid out. We often claim to understand this, but do we truly practice what we preach? Genuine acknowledgment also entails appreciating others' fears, misconceptions, and barriers. We shouldn't disregard their doubts; after all, every successful partnership begins with curiosity.

Let's break free from society's constraints and unlock the true potential that is so unique to our business model. By embracing authenticity, acknowledging others wholeheartedly, and overcoming obstacles, we can write our own stories of success and make our dreams a reality.

In our ever-evolving technological world, it's easy to overlook the most powerful tool at our disposal for building meaningful connections. It isn't a witty phrase or a flashy gadget. It is not found in a single phrase you will utter. It's you. Yes, you hold the key to unlocking the full potential of connection.

While technology may be advancing at an unprecedented pace, the fundamentals of engagement remain the same. It's the human element that truly matters. High touch wins over high tech every time. Authenticity trumps artificial intelligence. Your smile, your tone, your gestures - they hold immense power in shaping any interaction.

In a world where virtual communication has become the norm, it's important to remember that these essential elements of connection can still be utilized. Show up to Zoom meetings with your camera on, send voice memos instead of written texts, and don't forget to smile when you're on Facebook Live.

Embrace the power of connection. Utilize your inherent ability to customize every communication and foster genuine connections that transcend technology. You possess the ultimate key to forging lasting relationships in an increasingly digital world. As we work together to make greater connections, it won't always be an easy path. It requires us to be humble enough to acknowledge different perspectives, learn from those who have contrasting styles from us, and adopt new and challenging ideas!

Together, we can achieve incredible things by expanding our mindset and embracing diverse perspectives. Each opportunity to adapt brings us closer to understanding one another. It's important to actively listen to those we perceive as different and validate their experiences. Our differences should not divide us, but rather serve as bridges to connection and growth. We are stronger when we come together, and it's our collective responsibility to represent an industry that positively impacts countless lives. Let's embrace the dreams we aspire to and forge meaningful connections with new individuals. Together, we can (and will) make a difference.

Coach's Notes: In building meaningful connections, prioritize listening, sharing authentically, and focusing on the person in front of you. Leverage the F.O.R.M. method as a conversation starter, discussing Family, Occupation, Recreation, and Motivation to find common ground. My friend Kevin exemplifies this through his global experiences, proving that connection transcends cultural and linguistic barriers. Be present in every conversation, whether it's face-to-face or through digital platforms, and remember the power of a genuine smile or a sincere question.

Your authenticity is your greatest asset in fostering connections that can lead to lasting business relationships. Always approach interactions with an open heart and mind, ready to learn from each person's unique story.

"It's not about balancing your life, it's about balancing your mind despite the chaos."

— Author Unknown

MISTY LAVERTU

- Quickly embraced the industry, finding a sense of belonging.

- Achieved over 7 figures in Network Marketing (NWM) career.

- Led teams of hundreds of thousands, fostering numerous six-figure earners and thousands of high-level earners.

- Consistently ranked in top ten recruiters and earned all available incentive trips.

- Developed exclusive VIP coaching programs, guiding over 10,000 clients.

- Sought-after speaker and trainer in NWM and personal development, recognized for visionary leadership, storytelling, and transparent coaching.

In the fast-paced world of network marketing, where the pursuit of success is typically accompanied by a whirlwind of activity, it is essential to keep things simple and clear so that they can be duplicated. To thrive in the profession of network marketing, putting into practice simple strategies that are easy to understand and implement is not only necessary; but also, vital to achieving long term success.

As we break down the following strategies, my objective is to not only provide a road map for you but also to help individuals navigate the business with ease. My aim is to support you in cultivating an environment that fosters the learning necessary for creating *duplicatable simplicity*, along with the fundamental skills required for sustained growth and success.

I am going to share with you five tried and tested methods that have been around and utilized for a very long time. Each one of these steps have impacted me and my business over the years. Often, simply having the opportunity to hear something in a new way and at a different time can make all the difference. Sometimes, it is exactly what we need to turn the "*Chaos to Calm*".

Coach's Notes: Misty, with her seven-figure success in network marketing, underscores the power of simplicity and clarity in strategies for long-term success. As she unfolds her five proven methods, the focus is on creating easily duplicable processes that foster both individual growth and team development. Her approach aims to transform the often chaotic journey into a structured path of calm and steady progress. By prioritizing simplicity in strategies, Misty not only guides us through the foundational skills necessary for success but also emphasizes the importance of a learning environment conducive to growth. Let's dive into these strategies with the goal of mastering the art of simplification for sustained success in network marketing.

1. The Art of Time Management

Prospecting, team training, customer interactions, and other tasks are just a few of the many duties that network marketers frequently have to balance. The ability to efficiently manage time ensures that important tasks are attended to without causing overwhelm to oneself or one's team. This includes setting aside time for reaching out to new prospects, inviting, generating leads, the completion of follow-ups, and personal growth in order to maintain focus and concentration and reduce chaos.

When I first got started in NWM years ago, I was what some would call "ignorance on fire". I had an extreme drive, a desire for helping others and a complete love for my product and company. I was thriving in my new profession and excited to take on the world. As my team grew, I found that responsibilities increased as well and I was dealing with people and situations I had never dealt with before. The excitement I once felt was suddenly replaced by stress. I struggled every day to keep track of my hectic schedule, which included replying to messages and emails, making phone calls, following up, attending monthly trainings and conferences, planning meetings and the added responsibilities of working with a rapidly expanding team. There were moments when the lines between my personal and professional lives blurred, and I became frustrated and irritated without recognizing it.

It came to the point where I realized something had to change. I learned about time management from one of my upline business partners. She guided me on how she operated her business for over twenty years and was able to love her work while keeping clear boundaries. I began keeping track of everything I did on a daily basis. We studied it together, and she helped me in organizing my plan. We prioritized all the things I needed to do in order of importance. With her assistance and coaching, I was able to completely alter both my timetable and my approach. I started setting aside time for the most important tasks. I began to understand where and when my attention needed to be focused. By making this minor change, I was able to remove the distractions and learn to delegate the tasks that no longer fit into my time constraints. My days became more structured, my overall productivity increased, I was able to focus on the task at hand, and the best part was that my joy returned, and I once again had a vibrant team.

My undeveloped time management skills no longer posed a problem for me. Team members observed a shift and wanted to know what had changed. Many of them had the desire to improve their time management skills as well.

As our team began to achieve milestones together, we noticed an increase in customers and business partners. To this day, "The Art of Time Management" remains a defining moment in my NWM journey.

2. Communication: Embracing Transparency

For your network marketing business to truly thrive, this serves as a fundamental practice. The importance of communication cannot be overstated, whether it is with your team, customers, business partners and company. Ask yourself, "Do they have a clear understanding of the company's vision, the benefits of the products, and the pay plan?" By encouraging clear communication practices, this will reduce the likelihood of confusion and boost the level of productivity among the team. Your life and the success of your business will both increase by a factor of ten once you have achieved mastery of communication.

Several years ago, I had the opportunity to work with and learn from a woman who possessed the most pleasant demeanor I had ever encountered. For the purpose of the story, we'll refer to her as Elizabeth. Her ability to seamlessly connect with prospective customers and potential business partners was something I had never witnessed before. Her command of how she spoke was so advanced and eloquent that at times people would mimic her word for word and try to learn how to say it just like her. Her strengths were recognized by everyone, including me.

"*We are often told in NWM, find someone that you admire and model your business after that person.*" She was this person for me.

During a period of time when my team was experiencing rapid growth, we were facing significant communication challenges. Misunderstandings occurred, incorrect information was being shared and our overall message became unclear. These communication gaps caused uncertainty about our strategies and objectives. After observing what was going on in my organization, Elizabeth said that she had witnessed multiple situations within the team where a lack of communication was the primary source of the frustration.

We had a number of really genuine conversations and it became clear that I was not presenting my team with adequate information. We reflected on the previous few months and discussed some of the challenges that my team had faced. An overwhelming majority of the problems were caused by a lack of communication. So, in order to improve communication, I embraced the opportunity to actively participate and learn from Elizabeth. We worked together to update the training material, ensuring they were clear, concise, and easy to understand.

With this new, basic, yet powerful incite, I began reaching out to my leaders for open conversations. We held weekly team conference calls (yeah, this dates me) with the leaders to ensure communication was clear.

My entire team began to shift as a result of these changes, causing the overall dynamics to shift as well. Clear and transparent communication helped to establish relationships and trust among team members. The entire group agreed on the team's aim and direction, and they were all excited. The team thrived, goals were met and everyone celebrated their success.

Learning how to communicate is a skill that *CAN* be learned. However, if you interact with people on a daily basis, this is a skill that *MUST* be learned.

Coach's Notes: Misty's emphasis on communication as a cornerstone for success in network marketing is spot-on. Her approach, underscored by her experiences and the story of Elizabeth, highlights the power of embracing transparency.

My experience aligns with Misty's: Clear, open communication forms the backbone of any thriving network marketing business. It's not just about conveying information; it's about building trust, reducing confusion, and aligning your team towards common goals. The tale of Elizabeth's influence and the subsequent shifts in Misty's team underscore a crucial point: Communication skills are not innate but can be developed with intention and practice. By adopting practices such as regular team calls and revising training materials for clarity, you can foster a culture of transparency and inclusivity. Misty's narrative validates the critical role communication plays in network marketing and serves as a practical guide to elevating your business through improved interactions and shared understanding.

3. Blueprints of Success: Routines for Achieving your Goals

If you want to duplicate your success in network marketing, implementing established systems is helpful. In other words, create a blueprint. In addition to getting started guidelines, training modules, sales scripts, and follow-up techniques, these systems may also provide follow-up strategies that are simple enough for your team members to learn. The implementation of systems results in increased consistency, decreased confusion, and a more ordered workflow, all of which contribute to effective routines that help to achieve success for your entire team.

A few years back, a core group of my team were discussing how the workflow was progressing inside the organization. It became clear very quickly that a shift was needed. One of my business partners indicated that she was having a lot of trouble maintaining consistent sales, and her team was having difficulty duplicating what they were doing. We went back to the beginning and had an open discussion about what was and wasn't working. At the end of the meeting, we concluded that there were insufficient consistent systems in place to keep people focused and on target.

Positive results were immediately apparent following the implementation of the systems. We created training modules, scripts, and a step-by-step guide for efficient prospecting and follow-ups. Aside from planning, it was also important to have established specific procedures that had proven successful in the past. It was necessary for the team to have a plan for success.

When the team started implementing these systems, it became simple to duplicate their efforts. The newly engaged individuals on the team discovered that they had been equipped with the resources and information necessary to begin their journey with confidence.

Due to the fact that they had a structured road map to follow, they no longer experienced the feeling of being lost during the initial, chaotic days of getting started. Consistent procedures not only simplified the onboarding process, but also ensured that every member of the team followed "the how to" in the same way.

Systems evolved over the course of weeks and years in response to the feedback we received from the team. Fine-tuning the processes and introducing new techniques while maintaining the integrity of the fundamental concepts was simple and straightforward. The true commitment to the unified processes that emerged revealed the new structure's transformative impact. Having systems in place that are both easily replicated and scalable, allowed the team to focus on income producing activities and in turn left them feeling successful and empowered.

4. Reflect, Reframe & Thrive: The Power of Mindfulness

Managing the pressure to meet targets, achieve goals, deal with setbacks, and face rejection are all common obstacles that are encountered in network marketing. Individuals can be prepared with the tools necessary to address these issues with resilience by engaging in mindfulness practices and stress management techniques.

Meditation, exercise, deep breathing, and quick breaks can all help to reduce stress. You should encourage yourself and your team to engage in stress-relieving activities, as this will help you establish a more positive and focused mentality. Keep in mind that the less chaotic the working environment is, the more productive it becomes.

The joy and passion that we have for our business can frequently be overshadowed by stressful conditions. We can save a significant amount of time and effort by recognizing the need for an upgrade or shift in the way that we conduct our daily method of operation.

The chaos can be brought under control by incorporating moments of mindfulness throughout the day, such as a few minutes of deep breathing, a walk or a quick meditation session. When it comes to productivity and team management, it is essential that we first take care of ourselves. In order to renew our brains and bodies, we need to establish limits and boundaries, make time for rest and exercise, and engage in enjoyable activities. Taking short breaks during hectic days, emphasizing the significance of mental clarity and stress reduction, has proven to be incredibly effective on multiple occasions. I have used these strategies; the benefits are real and the results have proven beneficial time and again. Setting limits is not always easy, but it is a critical step toward leadership development.

This is one of the most significant things I've incorporated into my own personal business. I've often wondered how people don't burn out from the amount of work they take on, connections, meetings, calls and presentations. Many of us have been influenced by the hustle culture, which maintains that if we are not always full on, we aren't and never will be successful. I reached a point where I wasn't feeling aligned with what I was doing and I realized that if I didn't step back and take a break, my business and personal life would suffer. Giving myself permission was something I had heard of before, but I never felt it applied to me or my current circumstances. After reaching out to different leaders and mentors I allowed myself to step back, halt, breathe, get a massage, read a book and just simply be. For two days, I did nothing business-related; instead, I focused on clearing my mind and refocusing on what made me happy and fueled my purpose. It didn't take long for me to remember I truly loved what I did and couldn't wait to get back with my team. What a powerful lesson.

I began talking about this more, and as I shared its importance with my team, I saw that many others needed to learn how to give themselves permission as well. We had a conversation within the team and encouraged it throughout. This resulted in an increase in morale, as well as a reduction in frustration and setbacks. Mastering this simple but incredibly crucial skill has helped to develop resilience.

Over time, deeper connections were formed, trust and commitment among team members became more obvious, sales increased, and the organization as a whole succeeded. This served as confirmation and a reminder that achievement and inner calm were not mutually exclusive ideals.

5. Learn & Adapt: Keys to Sustainable Success

New consumer behaviors, trends, methods, and technology are regularly introduced into the ever-changing world of network marketing. Cultivating an environment in your team that encourages lifelong education and learning is an essential component of a team that stays on track. Investing in online courses, attending industry events and seminars in order to keep current is a recommended and smart business strategy.

Implementing what you've learned and remaining adaptable, allows you to make adjustments as needed. This allows you to maintain a competitive advantage while minimizing the disruption caused by unexpected changes in the company and the economy.

This one feels personal to me. Many people in my life, including friends, family, business partners and even some acquaintances, have told me "You're intense." My response was "Thank You". Of course, they don't mean it as a compliment, but that's precisely how I choose to hear it.

I was fourteen years old when I attended my first leadership retreat and fell in love with learning. I had no real knowledge that personal development was a thing at that age, but looking back, it was, and I believe that spending time at that weekend retreat prepared me to do what I do now. I can vividly recall the things we did to develop strength, resilience and drive.

I have had a lot of success throughout the years. However, the major shift occurred when I began attending team events, monthly meetings, regional and global conferences, and industry-wide conventions. Learning and improvement became an obsession. I consumed everything I could get my hands on, books, podcasts and audiobooks became my addiction.

Participating in seminars, reading, listening to podcasts, and watching videos on YouTube all became major sources of my energy. The concept of working with mentors became one that was accepted and celebrated. Changes occurred in my business environment as a result of the incorporation of new information, the implementation of strategies, and the utilization of social media platforms, and because I spent time learning and adapting, my business not only expanded, but thrived.

With the passing of time, it became clear that the landscape of NWM was changing yet again and because I had spent years studying, learning, growing and mastering new skills, I was able to adapt. I began sharing my experience with my entire organization. Since then, it became expected, without question, that my team would have an internal learning culture. I implemented training sessions on a regular basis, as well as consistently encouraging my team to keep up with the latest advances and trends.

As a result of their dedication to learning, the team began to feel more confident and adaptable. There was ample evidence of the outcomes that resulted from my commitment to sharing the ongoing strategy of learning and adapting. New customers, new business partners, new leaders and of course several new ranks within my organization.

Staying one step ahead is an effective approach in and of itself. Learning new things and adjusting to changing circumstances is not a choice in NWM; rather, it is a necessary component for success in a dynamic and competitive industry. You give yourself and your team the capacity to negotiate the industry's frequently unpredictable nature by focusing on what works.

In addition, creating a collaborative and supportive culture within your network marketing team can significantly improve desired outcomes. Encouraging open communication, sharing best practices, and cultivating a sense of togetherness among team members can create a vibrant and thriving community. This collaborative spirit not only enhances the overall morale but also helps to the overall performance of the team. As individuals engage in meaningful interactions, exchange valuable insights, and collectively work towards common goals, the synergy generated becomes a driving force for long-term growth and performance.

Harnessing the power of this ever-evolving strategy enables you to transform chaos into calm, resulting in a sense of balance and alignment in your life. As you navigate challenges and uncertainties, the ability to make this shift becomes your ultimate goal. Embracing this journey allows you to not only brave the storms, but also emerge stronger and more resilient. So, my friends, embrace the opportunity to create calm in the midst of chaos and see how profoundly it will impact every aspect of your life and business.

Coach's Notes: Misty emphasizes the critical roles of ongoing learning and adaptability for sustained success in network marketing. By continually embracing new knowledge and adjusting strategies, Misty has not only navigated changes within the industry but has also led her team to thrive. Implementing a culture of learning within your team can significantly boost confidence, adaptability, and performance. Her approach underlines that mastery in network marketing comes from both personal growth and fostering a collaborative team environment. Embrace learning and adapting as essential strategies to maintain a competitive edge and achieve long-term success.

"Always build the people, and the people will build your business."

— Author Unknown

DR. ANASTACIA LEWIS

- Network marketing professional since December 2019.
- Achieved five-figure earnings in the first two months; surpassed six-figure earnings within the first year.
- Leads a global team of nearly 200,000 individuals.
- Recognized as a Circle of Champions leader.
- Holds a doctorate in business and leadership.

Sit with the Winners the Conversation is Different

I am Dr. Anastacia Lewis, a proud native of the Bahamas. With fourteen years of experience in the networking space, I find joy in connecting with people as my background is banking and insurance. Leadership is my niche, and I am dedicated to making a positive impact in this realm. I have served my company for the entire fourteen years and have decided to share winning strategies for the masses.

My advice for any person stepping into this space is simply this: Sit with the winners, the conversation is different.

I'm going to give you twelve key pointers for winning, so get a pen and paper and buckle your seat belt we're going for a ride all the way to the top!

Point 1 Mindset Matters

Make up your mind to win from day one. Winners understand that the conversation they have with themselves first is the catalyst to the journey of entrepreneurship. It's not just about positive thinking; it's about cultivating a mindset that welcomes challenges as opportunities for growth. Instead of viewing obstacles as roadblocks, winners see them as stepping stones to success. This mindset shift sets the tone for resilience, perseverance, and a proactive approach to problem-solving. It's about rewiring our minds totally to focus on possibilities rather than limitations. Winners constantly feed their minds. Buy network marketing books and attend leadership conferences so that your mind is right to be able to overcome any hurdle. This mental fortitude will become the driving force behind your positive actions influencing how you approach prospects. Success in network marketing starts not just with what you do, but with the conversations you have with yourself. Deal with you first then seek out a key leader to learn from and let's get this journey started. You must listen to winners and not whiners. Winners navigate the course of action and steer you through the obstacles so you get the results you want. Being open, coachable and of course a good attitude gets you to the top. There's nothing new under the sun. Someone has set the bar high. Now you go ahead and duplicate.

Point 2 Focus on Value

What do I mean by this?

Winners focus on value and approach network marketing to building relationships and providing genuine value to customers and team members. Unlike traditional methods focused solely on product promotion, this approach prioritizes the creation of meaningful connections and delivering solutions that align with customers' needs. By establishing trust and rapport, network marketers can foster long-term loyalty and repeat business. In a value-centric model, the emphasis shifts from aggressive sales pitches to understanding and addressing the concerns of potential customers. This approach involves educating individuals about the benefits of products or services in a transparent manner, empowering them to make informed decisions. By positioning the product as a solution rather than a mere commodity, network marketers build credibility and authenticity. Furthermore, a value-centric approach extends to team building within the network marketing structure. You are a leader so you must prioritize mentoring, training, and supporting your team members to contribute to a positive and collaborative environment. This not only enhances the success of individual distributors but also strengthens the overall network. In essence, the value-centric approach transforms network marketing into a relationship-driven business. The value is in building people. Build the people and the people will build your business. Focus on the main thing. The solution is there and your commitment to serve. Keep the main thing the main thing.

Point 3 Learning is Continuous

When you show up you go up. If they don't appear they will disappear. In the dynamic landscape of direct selling, staying abreast of industry trends, marketing strategies, and product knowledge is paramount. Embracing a mindset of lifelong learning positions network marketers to adapt to changing market dynamics and evolving consumer preferences. Your job is to attend industry conferences, engage in webinars, travel with your company and read relevant literature to broaden your understanding of the field. Acquiring new skills, such as effective communication and digital marketing techniques, enables you to connect with a diverse audience. Moreover, staying informed about the products or services you promote enhances your credibility and empowers you to address customer queries with confidence. Remember, the network marketing landscape is dynamic, and those who invest in continuous learning not only stay competitive but also discover innovative ways to propel their businesses forward. Embrace education as a strategic tool, and you'll find that the journey of learning becomes a catalyst for sustained growth and professional fulfillment in the realm of network marketing. It takes real confidence and faith not only to stay abreast but some things we must also unlearn to relearn. Keep an open mind, things change quickly. You remain in that frame of mind and stick with positive people who force you to level up and focus on your personal brand and competence. It's not good enough just to be nice but functional globally. The work is yours and people who have achieved any level of success help you. They put the information in a book. Keep reading!

Coach's Notes: Dr. Anastacia Lewis showcases the essence of success in network marketing through mindset, value, and learning. She emphasizes starting with a winner's mindset, seeing challenges as steps to growth. Focusing on providing value over sales, she advises building genuine connections. Lastly, she highlights continuous learning as key to adapting and thriving in the ever-evolving industry. Her approach underscores the importance of resilience, authentic relationships, and lifelong education as pillars for sustained success. Lastly, she walks the walk with a team organization of over 200,000 members! She knows what she is doing.

Point 4 Create Authentic Relationships

Authentic relationships lie at the heart of successful network marketing business. Be yourself. People can tell when you are being fake. In this industry, building trust is not just a strategy; it's a fundamental necessity. Authenticity involves genuine connections, where network marketers prioritize understanding the unique needs and aspirations of their clients and team members. It's about more than transactions – it's about creating value and fostering a sense of teamwork and reciprocity. I help you and you help me. Authenticity resonates with people, as it transcends the typical sales pitch. Do not manipulate people to join you in business and spend excessive amounts of money just to help you get to the top, it backfires. When you approach interactions with sincerity, they build a foundation of trust that forms the basis of long-lasting relationships that goes beyond business and the industry. This approach not only leads to customer loyalty but also fuels the growth of a supportive network. Leaders who authentically support and mentor their teams create an environment where individuals feel valued and empowered. As a network marketer, embracing authenticity means being transparent about products or services, acknowledging limitations, and celebrating successes. Ultimately, the authenticity embedded in these relationships serves as a powerful catalyst, driving not only business success but also personal fulfillment and a positive reputation within the network marketing community. In a world saturated with marketing messages, authentic relationships stand out.

Point 5 Create Clear Goals

Setting clear goals is a foundational pillar for success in network marketing. Write down your goals every single month. If you can see it you can be it. Here's the thing: You must define both short-term and long-term objectives to create a structured and measurable path forward. Clarity in your goals allows you to articulate specific targets for sales, team growth, and personal development. Break down larger objectives into manageable tasks, making them more achievable and less overwhelming. This approach not only enhances focus but also fosters a sense of accomplishment as each milestone is reached. In the dynamic world of network marketing, setting clear goals enables adaptability. As you monitor your progress, you can adjust strategies, refine your approach, and pivot when necessary. Goals serve as motivation, driving you to push beyond comfort zones and capitalize on opportunities. Share your goals with your team to huddle. Make sure you initiate an intense sense of purpose and unity, aligning everyone toward a common vision. Regularly reassess and update your goals to reflect changing market conditions and personal growth otherwise you lose market share and credibility. This process ensures that your network marketing business remains alive, fresh and responsive. Ultimately, clear goals provide a framework for success, serving as a catalyst for continuous improvement, sustained motivation, and your team will realize and duplicate. You cannot want your team to do what you do not do. Intentionally write it down.

Point 6 Keep it Moving Don't Stop

Consistent action!!!!! Events, events, events!!! Winners understand that it's not the sporadic bursts of effort but the steady, relentless commitment to tasks that yield significant results. In the world of network marketing, where building relationships and trust takes time, the conversation shifts from occasional sprints to a marathon of consistent and intentional actions. This means daily engagement, whether it's reaching out to prospects, creating valuable content, or refining one's skills. Consistency builds momentum, and consistency makes you heavy and a credibility adds to elevating your brand which creates a ripple effect that fosters growth. When you consistently show up, your audience begins to recognize your commitment and reliability. Out of sight out of mind!! It's about setting routines and habits that align with your goals. So my advice is to get an accountability partner who will hold your feet to the fire to force you to level up in activity. Winners in network marketing understand that success is not an overnight phenomenon nor a lottery, but a culmination of persistent, disciplined efforts. People know when you are serious about your business. In the relentless pursuit of success, it's not the intensity of action but the consistency that transforms aspirations into tangible achievements. Believe it or not when you start and stop you push yourself back six months to a year and it takes time to get your momentum back. Sooooo keep it moving, don't stop!!!!!

Point 7 Sometimes You Have to Shift Adaptability

What is adaptability? Having an open mind to understand that things change and sometimes you have to shift it or you will get left behind. Winners in this field understand that the conversation revolves around being flexible, agile, and responsive to change. In an industry where trends shift, algorithms evolve, and consumer behaviors transform, adaptability becomes a strategic advantage. The ability to pivot, adjust strategies, and embrace emerging opportunities is what sets apart those who thrive. Be around team members who are constantly working so you hear when things shift. Stay connected to your company. Winners engage in a continuous conversation with the ever-changing market, acknowledging that what worked yesterday may not be effective tomorrow. They eagerly adopt new technologies, stay abreast of industry shifts, and evolve with the demands of the audience.

This adaptability extends beyond external factors to personal growth. Embracing change is not just a survival strategy but a catalyst for innovation and long-term success. Ignoring industry changes and market changes is like hammering nails in your coffin and you to be buried. The conversation we all need to have with ourselves and our teams is one of resilience, curiosity, and a commitment to staying ahead of the curve. In a realm where adaptability is synonymous with staying relevant and ahead of the game. Winners not only navigate change but thrive in it, So we must have an open mind and keep our ears to the ground to gather the relevant information using each shift as a springboard for continued success in the ever-evolving world of network marketing.

Point 8 Leaders Show Up

Leadership presence is the heartbeat of success in network marketing. You want to lead a team you cannot be absent. Winners understand that the conversation they project, both verbally and non-verbally, shapes the confidence and trust of their team. If people don't respect your leadership they simply don't listen to you. It goes beyond titles; it's about embodying qualities that inspire and motivate. A strong leadership presence involves clarity in communication, transparency in decision-making, and a genuine commitment to the well-being and growth of the team. Again I say find a leader who you admire and learn so everyone feels heard, valued, and empowered. Leaders with a commanding presence lead by example, demonstrating the work ethic, integrity, and resilience they expect from their team. You cannot expect your team to do what you are not willing to do as accountability goes both ways up and down. This authenticity resonates within the network, establishing a foundation of trust and loyalty. The ability to navigate challenges with grace and to celebrate successes with humility is woven into the leadership conversation. It's about setting a tone that encourages innovation, continuous learning, and a shared vision. In network marketing, where relationships are pivotal, a leader's presence becomes the catalyst for unity, motivation, and the realization of collective goals. Leadership presence is not just about being in charge; it's about making a positive, lasting impact on the individuals who make up the network, creating an environment where everyone can thrive and succeed together.

Coach's Notes: Leadership presence, as highlighted, is crucial in network marketing. It's defined not by titles but by actions and attitudes that inspire trust and motivation. A leader must be visible, communicative, and genuinely committed to the team's growth. Emulating admired leaders, embodying work ethic, and fostering an environment of transparency and accountability are key. This approach builds a solid foundation of trust and loyalty, essential for navigating challenges and celebrating successes. Leadership is about impacting lives positively and creating a thriving community.

Point 9 Effective Communication

Effective communication serves as the lifeblood of success in network marketing. Winners recognize that the conversation they engage in, shapes the perception of their brand and the strength of their connections. In this dynamic field, where building relationships is paramount, effective communication goes beyond words; it involves active listening and understanding the needs of your team and customers. Clarity is the cornerstone – whether explaining the benefits of a product or outlining the vision for the team. They tailor their communication style to match the preferences of their audience, ensuring a genuine connection. Moreover, winners leverage various channels, from social media platforms to personalized messages, recognizing that diverse communication strategies reach a broader audience. What I've come to realize is the cultural differences in communication as this is a global business so you must really foster great relationships so that you are not offending your leaders in different countries. Timeliness are also crucial; in a fast-paced industry, responding promptly and maintaining open lines of communication builds trust. The conversation revolves around building bridges, not just making transactions. Effective communication in network marketing is a two-way street, fostering engagement and collaboration. By mastering the art of articulation and listening, winners create an environment where ideas flow freely, relationships flourish, and the network becomes a community bound by shared goals and effective communication which reveals what went wrong and what is going right. The real deal is keep talking until you figure everything out.

Point 10 You Need a Coach/Mentorship

Mentorship is a huge deal for success in network marketing. This is your support and training ground for success. Winners understand that the conversation goes beyond personal achievements; it involves a commitment to both seeking guidance and providing support. Embracing a mentorship mentality means acknowledging that there is always room for growth and that learning from those who have navigated the path before can be transformative. Winners actively seek mentorship, valuing the insights and experiences of seasoned professionals. Simultaneously, they embrace the responsibility of being mentors themselves, fostering an environment where knowledge is shared, and growth is nurtured. The Law of Recognition speaks to acknowledging whose voice you should be listening to. The conversation within a mentor is one of continuous learning, constructive feedback, and a shared commitment to each other's success. It's about more than just transactions; it's about building meaningful relationships within the network. Sometimes it extends beyond formal arrangements; it becomes a culture where collaboration thrives, and success is a collective achievement. Winners understand that the strength of the network lies in its interconnected support system, where individuals uplift each By embracing mentorship not only to accelerate their personal growth. Mentorship sometimes is one of the hardest things to do especially for professionals coming from their specific fields. They have experienced success already and they feel this industry is the same but sadly it's not.

Point 11 Accept the Challenges

Embracing challenges is a defining characteristic of winners in network marketing. Like any other business there will be challenges. I do not know of any person in business who does not encounter some type of challenge or drama. The conversation they have with adversity is not one of avoidance but of opportunity. Challenges are seen as stepping stones, not stumbling blocks. Winners understand that each hurdle presents a chance to learn, innovate, and refine their approach. Rather than being deterred by setbacks, they welcome them as catalysts for growth. The conversation revolves around resilience, acknowledging that the path to success in network marketing is not a straight line. Instead, it's a journey filled with twists and turns, requiring adaptability and a positive mindset. Winners don't fear challenges; they see them as indicators of progress. When faced with obstacles, their dialogue is focused on solutions and strategic adjustments. This approach not only propels personal development but also inspires confidence within their network. Words by the late Dr. Myles Munroe, one of my mentors, "Problems are an opportunity for wealth." By embracing challenges openly, winners cultivate a culture where everyone understands that overcoming difficulties is an integral part of the journey. The conversation shifts from complaining about problems to collectively finding solutions. In network marketing, challenges are not roadblocks but opportunities to shine. Winners use adversity as a tool for self-discovery and a catalyst for strengthening the bonds within the network. In the face of challenges, the dialogue is not one of defeat but of determination, resilience, and an unwavering commitment to achieving success.

Coach's Notes: Embracing challenges as opportunities for growth is crucial in network marketing, a principle I've discussed in *The Game of Conquering*. Every obstacle presents a chance to learn, innovate, and strengthen your resolve, mirroring the journey of any successful business person. Dr. Myles Munroe's wisdom, 'Problems are an opportunity for wealth,' underscores this mindset. It's about shifting the conversation from avoidance to proactive problem-solving, fostering a team culture where challenges are met with resilience and creativity. This approach not only propels individual development but also solidifies trust and unity within the team, proving that facing adversity head-on is a testament to progress and a key driver of success.

Point 12 Celebrate Success & Go Global

One of my favorite topics Going global in network marketing. I'm excited because I have built a global team. A transformative step that requires a strategic conversation. Winners understand that expanding beyond borders means tapping into diverse markets and adapting to varying cultures. The conversation revolves around making money from anywhere around the world while appreciating the uniqueness of each market. The conversation about success is not just about personal achievements but about the collective triumph of the entire team spanning continents. How do we go global? It happens through technology, social media platforms and also organically. Every country has someone from another country who has settled.

Conversations and conversations events break the ice and foster building relationships and then partnerships. Advertise your business. You'll be shocked as to who is watching you. Your team members also allow you to go global conversation becomes a symphony of diverse voices harmonizing towards a common goal, creating a network that thrives on global collaboration and celebrates the success of each member as a victory for the entire global community. The real deal in network marketing is a global team.

I have so many more points to share as this is an ongoing learning process. All in all Winners help you to focus so sit with them, have lunch, have dinner and in all that you do have fun in your business as you continue to build your empire!!!!!!

Love you all,
I'll see you at the top (and at the bank).

"Master yourself."

— Robbie Cornelius

MARGARET ANNE NEWSOME

- Joined Network Marketing in 1997 and built a global organization.
- Top 1% of two network marketing companies.
- Serial entrepreneur.
- Real Estate Broker/Investor.
- Speaker, Leadership Trainer, Personal Development Coach, Author.

The Art of Self-Sabotage

Simple steps to Break the Cycle, Get out of Your Own Way, and Master Success

Do you ever feel like you know what you should do, but you just can't seem to do it? Why is that? I've asked myself a gazillion times, "You know what to do, so why don't you just do it?" It sounds simple, right? I've looked everywhere for answers, and as it turns out, I'm the problem. I've been sabotaging myself and you probably have been too. It's time to figure out why we self-sabotage and how to stop this destructive behavior. There is a way to get out of your own way for good.

Self-sabotage is when your actions don't align with your goals. Self-sabotage can be both intentional and unintentional. It is usually an unconscious survival strategy. It's a way of protecting yourself. But protecting yourself from what?

Have you ever asked yourself what you are gaining by self-sabotaging? What function is your self-sabotaging serving? What are you protecting yourself from? Are you avoiding action because it's safer and easier to stay in your comfort zone? Are you avoiding fear? If so, fear of what? Fear of being out of your comfort zone? Fear of judgment? Fear of having to learn something new? Fear of failure? Or maybe fear of success? Or maybe it's fear of the unknown? Do you want to stop getting in your own way, but you just don't know how to do it? That was me. I went on a journey of discovery and this is what I found.

Self-sabotage isn't a one-size-fits-all. It appears in various types. Each type has its own unique challenges and pitfalls. Recognizing which type of self-sabotager you are is the first step toward breaking free from destructive patterns and reclaiming control of your life.

Let's take a look at some common types of self-sabotagers. Many people relate to more than one type. Which types fit you?

Coach's Notes: Margaret's exploration of self-sabotage is both crucial and all too rarely discussed in the context of professional and personal growth. This topic's significance lies in its universal applicability; nearly everyone has faced moments where their actions misalign with their ambitions, leading to frustration and stagnation. By confronting the underlying fears and motivations behind self-sabotage, Margaret provides invaluable insights into overcoming these barriers. Identifying and addressing the types of self-sabotage can unlock a path to success that many find elusive. This chapter serves as a vital guide for those ready to move beyond their limitations, offering clear strategies to break the cycle of self-sabotage and embrace a journey toward achieving their full potential.

Understanding the Types of Self-Sabotagers

1. **The Procrastinator**: Always putting things off until tomorrow? The procrastinator thrives on delay tactics, avoiding decisions and important tasks until the last possible moment. Procrastination leads to added stress, missed opportunities, and stunted growth.

2. **The Perfectionist**: Setting unrealistically high standards and fearing anything less than flawless, the perfectionist often finds themselves stuck in a cycle of self-doubt and indecision. The perfectionist can develop a fear of taking risks and trying new things, limiting progress. Embracing imperfection and prioritizing progress over perfection is the key to breaking free.

3. **The People-Pleaser**: Putting others' needs before their own, the people-pleaser struggles to say no and often sacrifices their own goals and well-being for the sake of approval. Learning to set boundaries and prioritize self-care is essential for overcoming this self-sabotaging tendency.

4. **The Self-Sabotaging Fixer**: Always swooping in to solve other people's problems, the self-sabotaging fixer neglects their own needs and goals in the process. Learning to prioritize personal growth and set healthy boundaries is crucial for breaking free from this pattern.

5. **The Critic**: Engaging in negative self-talk and constantly doubting their abilities, the critic undermines their own potential and achievements. Cultivating self-compassion and challenging negative thought patterns is essential for overcoming this self-sabotaging tendency.

6. **The Avoider**: Preferring to avoid challenges, uncomfortable situations, or difficult conversations, the avoider misses out on opportunities for personal and professional growth. Learning to confront and overcome challenges head-on is essential for breaking free from this pattern.

7. **The Martyr**: Taking on excessive responsibilities and neglecting their own well-being, the martyr often ends up feeling overwhelmed and burnt out. Learning to prioritize self-care and delegate tasks is crucial for overcoming this self-sabotaging tendency.

You may be wondering how to recognize when you are self-sabotaging. If you think you self-sabotage, ask yourself the following questions and answer them honestly:

Questions to Ask Yourself:

1. Is my behavior aligning with my goals?

   If not, what is stopping me from taking action to make my dreams come true?

2. Is my behavior aligning with values that I currently believe?

   If not, what is stopping me from taking actions that align with these values?

3. Do I feel uneasiness or discomfort when I progress? If yes, dig deeper:

   Is this discomfort based on what others told you that limited your aspirations?

   Is this discomfort based on a fear of failure and worry about looking foolish?

   Is this unease based on a fear of success?

4. Are you concerned with achieving more than you thought possible?

   If you do better or achieve more, do you believe success is more than you deserve?

Now that you understand some of the types of self-sabotagers, here are some things you can do to stop self-sabotage and reclaim your power:

Strategies to Combat Self-Sabotage

1. **Change the Thought Loop**: Thoughts-Feelings-Beliefs-Actions

   Interrupt self-sabotaging patterns by replacing negative thoughts with positive thoughts. Learn to reframe your thoughts and regulate emotions. Change begins with your thoughts. Thoughts become feelings. Feelings become beliefs and beliefs become actions. What you think over and over again becomes your subconscious autopilot. Train your brain to work in your favor. When negative thoughts creep in, replace those negative thoughts with positive thoughts. Don't accept negativity, reject it.

Here are a couple of tips to train your brain to work in your favor:

- Don't use "I should" statements. Sometimes feeling like you should do, act, or feel a certain way adds just enough pressure that you end up procrastinating or avoiding a responsibility or activity completely. Use words like "I will try my best...", "I can...", "I will...".

- Become aware of automatic negative thoughts (ANTs). These are your first thoughts when you have a strong feeling or reaction to something. Some examples include telling yourself "I'm not smart enough to do this", "I'm going to mess this up", "I don't fit in". Reframe your thoughts. Is there credible evidence for your thought? Is there credible evidence against your thought? Find an alternative for your original thought. Pretend like you are giving advice to a friend about their thoughts. What would you tell them? Learn to pause, check-in and reframe.

2. **Overcome Analysis Paralysis**: Combat inaction by doing ONE task at a time. Just do the ONE thing. Then do the next ONE thing. Celebrate small victories. Progress stems from taking the first step. You can't walk a mile without taking the first step.

3. **Recognize Behavior Patterns**: Understanding self-sabotaging tendencies is crucial. Procrastinators, perfectionists, people-pleasers, self-sabotaging fixers, critics, avoiders, and martyrs—identifying your archetype is the first step towards transformation. Recognize when you're falling into self-sabotaging patterns and redirect those behaviors.

Become aware of the behavior loop. The loop consists of cues, routines, and rewards. Learn to recognize cues of things that are getting you off track. Common cues that derail people are location, time, your current emotional state, the people around you, and your last action.

Pay attention to location cues. If you stop by the breakroom for a cup of coffee, do you immediately return to your desk to work, or do you get sucked into a long conversation with a co-worker and get derailed? Did you stop by Target on the way home for just one item and end up roaming around shopping for an hour for things you really don't need instead of heading to work on your goals? Resist locations that negatively impact your goals. Your last action is the thing you did before you sabotaged yourself. For example, did you hit snooze this morning and then rush to get out the door? Did you commit to something that is taking time away from working on your goals? Become aware of your choices. You are in control of yourself. Use the "If-then" plan. "If" you do this, "then" this will happen. Choose wisely.

Put routines in place and stick to them. Routines are key for staying on track. Have routines for your day from the time you wake up until you go to bed. When you establish a routine your brain can anticipate what is coming next. This reduces anxiety and stress. You won't have to work as hard to figure out what to do, you will just automatically know.

When making changes, start small. Choose something small that gets you a win, a small reward. Your brain will recognize this and will help tell you to do the task again to be rewarded again. Soon a new behavior will be learned in place of the old behavior. Once you have a new behavior, add on another one. If you fall off the wagon, don't beat yourself up. Just get up and keep going. Allow yourself grace and keep practicing. You will learn to recognize behavior patterns and make different choices that direct you towards your goals.

Coach's Notes: Margaret's insights into breaking the cycle of self-sabotage are incredibly straightforward and impactful. Her focus on changing the thought loop and tackling analysis paralysis provides a clear roadmap for those looking to get out of their own way.

The practical strategies she outlines, such as reframing negative thoughts and focusing on one task at a time, are essential tools for anyone ready to master success. Implementing these strategies, as Margaret suggests, is the key to transforming self-sabotage into self-empowerment. It's a reminder that the path to overcoming our biggest obstacles often starts with our mindset and daily actions.

4. **Embrace Imperfect Action**: Don't let the pursuit of perfection hold you back. Take imperfect action and course-correct along the way. Messy action is better than no action. Progress, not perfection, is the goal.

5. **Set Boundaries**: Learn to say no and prioritize your own needs and goals. Setting boundaries is essential for protecting your time and energy. Boundaries define what is acceptable and what is not. Know there is a difference between helping others and allowing yourself to take on other people's problems as an excuse to avoid working on your own goals. Protect your time. Stay clear and focused. Setting boundaries is a major part of any leader's skill set.

6. **Delegate**: Effective delegation goes hand in hand with setting boundaries. Delegation is important to make sure that you are not overloaded with tasks that others can handle. Taking on excessive responsibilities will lead to burnout. You can't do it all yourself and it is okay and oftentimes necessary to delegate.

   Sometimes people don't delegate because they don't want to burden others. This is a people-pleasing mentality, stop it! Many times people would be happy to help and support you if you will just ask. Sometimes people don't delegate because they don't want to let go of control of the task. Sometimes you may think it's faster to just do it yourself. Find the courage to delegate. Be specific about what you need. Provide a timeline that the task will take and provide the tools to complete the task. Make it easy for people to say yes. Finding the correct people to help complete tasks can free you up to work on your goals. Delegate tasks according to someone's skill level and time flexibility. Delegating, especially in seasons of busyness, can be a lifesaver.

7. **Practice Self-Compassion and Self-care**: Treat yourself with kindness and compassion. We all stumble and fall—it's how we pick ourselves back up that matters. Take care of yourself. Be sure you eat well, get adequate sleep, and exercise. Spend time in nature. Make time for quiet time to decompress, and make sure you have some fun!

8. **Seek Support**: Find yourself a supportive community. Surrounding yourself with a supportive community can make all the difference.

Supportive communities provide a safe and non-judgemental space for people to share their thoughts, feelings,and experiences without the fear of rejection or ridicule. A supportive community also provides a place for connection with others who are on a similar journey. It can be a place to help you feel less alone when navigating challenges.

These communities are especially important in the context of building self-esteem. It is helpful to be in a community with people who understand what you are going through. People in the community can truly help because they have been where you are. They can be an excellent source for guidance and encouragement.

A supportive community can also provide great practical help. Through sharing information, resources, or just giving a helping hand, community members come together and pool their collective knowledge to offer valuable aid to everyone in the community.

As you see others in the community make progress in their journey, it becomes a source of hope and inspiration. Witnessing others grow can instill a profound belief that you can do it too!

Embrace Change and Take Responsibility

Overcoming self-sabotage requires self-awareness, choices for change, and implemented action. Acknowledge that there will be discomfort along the way. Embrace the challenges; it's a sign you're headed in the right direction. As network marketers and entrepreneurs, mastering self-sabotage is key to unlocking our full potential.

Be real with yourself. Ask yourself, "What are you gaining by staying stuck?" Answer that question honestly. Face your fears. Challenge your excuses. Start believing in yourself. Take action. You are worth it.

Coach's Notes: Margaret rounds off her discussion on overcoming self-sabotage with a powerful call to embrace change and take responsibility. Her emphasis on self-awareness and the willingness to face discomfort as indicators of progress is particularly resonant. As she rightly points out, overcoming self-sabotage is not just about recognizing destructive patterns but actively choosing to change and taking steps towards that change.

Her closing words serve as a reminder that the journey towards overcoming self-sabotage and realizing our full potential begins with an honest self-assessment, facing our fears, and making a committed effort to change. This message is especially relevant in the network marketing and entrepreneurship space, where self-belief and action can significantly impact success. Margaret's guidance provides a blueprint for not just recognizing self-sabotage but also for actively dismantling it to unlock our true capabilities.

"Don't put a period, where God put a comma. He can help you repurpose your mess and turn it into a message to build a Masterpiece"

– Author Unknown

JULIA THORNHILL

- A former marketing director and Navy SEAL and parents of 2 littles, Brandon and Julia are pioneering a faith-based team spanning over 20 countries, fostering 100+ organic 6-figure earners and distributing nearly $100 million in commissions to their organization.

- They are celebrated for hosting a multitude of transformational events for their team, including marriage retreats, women's empowerment gatherings, masterminds, exotic retreats and leadership bootcamps.

- Achieving their company's highest leadership retention, they are renowned for revolutionary systems and a bold, vibrant culture of parents who love to travel the world and experience life with their kids.

- Raised nearly $1 million for humanitarian causes, combating human trafficking, and aiding hungry families worldwide.

Retention with Intention

Imagine crafting a business that not only weathers the storms of recessions, pandemics, and world crises but emerges stronger and more resilient.

Here's the deal – you can learn the skills, teach the tactics, and sprinkle in mindset wisdom, but it's the infusion of intention that keeps the growth flowing. This isn't just about business; it's about the people. It's about painting a canvas of possibilities, reigniting dreams, and holding space for others to dream again. It's about believing in their potential even before they catch a glimpse of it. Trust me, once you believe, you can lead. In a world full of mundane, underwhelming zoom calls and rah rah old school hype, the need for more intention could be just the solution.

Hi friends! My name is Julia Thornhill (call me, Jules!) and I'm here to share a piece of my heart with you. My husband Brandon and I have been instrumental in nurturing over 100 six-figure earners and multiple seven-figure achievers in the realm of network marketing. We have held the highest retention in leadership for years in multiple countries and have helped families earn almost $100 million online in the product space. 98% of those people did not have any experience. Yes, we built everything from scratch. No handouts, no big business given, nothing. Just raw creation from the ground up.

In our world, it's not about transactions; it's about transformations. Which brings me to what I believe is a bit unique behind the scenes and can help ANY organization increase retention after being a part of the best masterminds in our industry.

This includes:
Events
Committees
Unified Mission

All with MASSIVE intention behind them, Jesus with a dash of Tony Robbins.

My background is in marketing and my husband was a Navy SEAL for twelve years. He grew up in a trailer park, I grew up on food stamps. We lacked mentorship in all areas of our life. To date, we have invested about $500k in personal development and over the last eight years we found a good balance between each other. I, Julia, am the events, visionary, systems-obsessed leader and my husband is the hard coach; the hammer with a huge heart and the one that says the things someone may not want to hear but needs to hear to become the best version of themselves.

We've been asked countless times, "What are you doing differently?" So, let me spill the beans on what's uniquely brewing behind the scenes, infused with a lot of Jesus and a dash of Tony Robbins.

On almost every event or team call, our goal (outside of just helping others making money or getting results on products) is to help people in seven specific areas of their life. These are not mine, they are based on Tony Robbins *7 Areas of Constant Growth for an Extraordinary Life*.

So let's break it down and how this can apply to your business:

- Health and Vitality
- Mind and Meaning
- Love and Relationships
- Productivity and Performance
- Career and Business
- Wealth and Lifestyle
- Leadership and Impact

I believe that people can make 6-figures a month in this industry but if they're not growing, if they don't feel valued, if they're a part of something bigger than themselves or if they're not walking away from your calls, events, and interaction they won't last.

Coach's Notes: Julia Thornhill, whom I know well and have immense respect for, exemplifies what it means to be a solid leader in network marketing. Her approach sets a benchmark for creating not just a successful business, but a thriving community.

Julia and her husband Brandon's journey from humble beginnings to nurturing over 100 six-figure earners is an unreal example of their commitment to personal development and leadership.

Their focus on transforming lives across the *7 Areas of Constant Growth, shows the importance of development in achieving extraordinary success.* Their strategies, emphasizing events, committees, and a unified mission, all driven by massive intention, is a powerful blueprint for any organization looking to improve retention and foster a culture of continuous growth. Julia's narrative is a reminder that the heart of network marketing lies in the people and the potential transformations within them, urging leaders to believe in their team's potential, even before they see it in themselves.

So what I want to do first is to break down a few ways we help our team improve in those seven areas of their life in regards to events for each category. Let's dive in, shall we?

1. **Health and Vitality**: We're in the mental wellness space, so that probably won't align with your world too so for those of you in different niches, consider incorporating health initiatives like drinking a gallon of water a day or the seventy five hard challenge for your teams. You could even start your daily calls with an attitude of gratitude.

2. **Mind and Meaning**: Lots of mindset training for this one Monday through Friday for ten minutes before our daily calls every day. We also make sure our monthly regional calls always have a session on this. Let's be honest, this business is 90% mindset, 10% skill set. You can have the best tools, apps, gadgets and training but if their mindset isn't right and they are going into everything you're training on with the wrong intention then it's a waste of time. It's like a ship without a compass.

3. **Love and Relationships**: During our launch process people are assigned mentorship, accountability partners and through our events they build the most amazing friendships. Our marriage retreats, leadership bootcamps and family experiences heavily create this more than any zoom can. Proximity is power. Experiences are everything. This is one of my favorite parts about this business, it's the conversations I've had with my team around a campfire in Jackson hole or on a yacht in Dubai about our kids (preferably all our kids are there too). This is what I always pictured, building a community you can trust your own kids around. Trips and experiences around the world and memories created. I'll dive more into events shortly.

4. **Productivity and Performance**: We like to do time management training (especially with kids). Lots of different tools, training on A.I. and accountability challenges. I believe that you also need to build the business with the things that bring you joy, first. So rather than put all the things you need to do to move the needle forward, instead, put all the things that bring you joy. For example, write down in your calendar this week the things that make you happy. For example: Skiing, playing with your kids, date night, the gym, self-care, etc. After those are booked, then put in what needs to get done for your business. This will allow you to avoid resentment, burnout or push things behind that are important to your overall mental wellness and happiness. The happier you are the better you'll perform!

5. **Career and Business**: We are all relevant here! We all run businesses, however, there are more effective ways to do that. Running a business does not mean burn out. Running a business means being efficient with your time with the little time you have, especially if you are building it around a traditional job. In this life factor, this is where your mission and vision can come in that I'll get to. This is where people believing they are a part of something bigger than themselves can contribute. This is where getting your teams involved in all the moving pieces it takes to run can aid in them feeling valued and growing. This is also where your events can come in to play to help improve their overall life in so many ways.

6. **Wealth and Lifestyle**: For wealth, we do yearly wealth summits and tax education for this one. The goal is not to teach someone how to make ten thousand dollars a month and spend it all, the goal is to create more FREEDOM. If someone earned a company car, it doesn't mean they go get the car, you know? For lifestyle, we do paid-for trips to Dubai and spoil our six-figure earners or anyone who's earned over $100k with red bottoms or custom suits. You can get creative here. It could even be heavily promoting your company trips. Don't overthink it. I also believe you should heavily involve your kids if you're a parent. They should know the ranks and when you hit every milestone. Make it their promotion too. Every month or two go do something fun! It can be as simple as going to get ice cream and camping or as extravagant as flying to Europe (if it's in your budget). We like to go on trips every 90 days. Not team trips (those are fun too) but trips that WE plan as a family. This allows them to be involved in the growth and also be involved in the milestones. If you have older kids, write down what they would want to do and throw it in a hat - the more you can get them involved, the better !

7. **Leadership and Impact/Contribution**: Outside of our leadership retreats and bootcamps, this is where our committees come into play so keep reading.

Now that we've tackled the seven areas intentionally, let's dive right in and start with EVENTS.

To date, We've hosted a plethora, hundreds – from grand conventions that cost over $100,000 to intimate team gatherings. The size doesn't matter; it's the impact that echoes. Here's the playbook from largest to smallest in regards to attendance:

1. **Team Only Event at our Company Convention**: We always have our own breakout and launch new tools, incentives, do recognition, etc.

2. **Our Yearly Team Event aka Wealth Summit and Branding Workshop**: It's like a convention just for your team. There have been times where our team event was bigger than convention! It's been titled wealth summit for several years and then tacking on a sub category has been new.

3. **Leadership Bootcamp**: I love the breakdown, breakthrough and build up technique. Think adult summer camp but ten times better.

4. **Customer Appreciation**: We have executed several events, from wellness workshops to renting out entire water parks - we want our customers to feel a part of our mission and to feel appreciated. The water park was a blast since our community involved tons of parents so it was a great day to hang out with all of our families. We set up stations so our customers could experience products they may never have had and we got our partners all involved to play an important role in executing such a unique experience!

5. **Team Qualifier Retreat**: These are usually at exotic locations for just our team built around corporate incentives. Try not to work against the company, only complement it. For example, if the company has an incentive with a points system they are tracking, work in similar qualifications and when they hit a bigger milestone, you offer a trip!

6. **Marriage Retreats**: I believe the family unit is more important than ever and since the majority of our top leaders are couples, we've run several to strengthen their marriages. Our most recent was in Park City and was over valentines weekend.

7. **Masterminds**: This is for our CEO council and some of our Head of committees. We dive into everything from systems, events and challenges to what's mapped out that year. I've brought in catering, massage therapists and photographers for brand shoots.

8. **Core Family Events**: This is an event for all our top earners and their kids. I.e. We rented a chalet in deer valley, went skiing and catered the weekend. This is more of a fun event to just create memories. There isn't much business talk here even though it's hard to not because we love what we do so much, but this is more an event to get to know our team's families and their kids more. The overall goal is to just create memories together.

9. **Charity Events**: I believe that if you're blessed, be a blessing. Our team has raised over half a million dollars to fight human trafficking and feed families. Some ideas you can take on that we've also done is rally behind a charity your leaders or team votes on. We have also done local charity events and seasonal events around the holidays to give back, from toy and clothes drives to volunteering at local charities. You can get different countries and cities in your team to have a friendly competition on most donations raised. Tis the season to always give back!

10. **Virtual Events**: From Women's workshops to Mental Wellness Masterclasses, we pack a ton of value into them and are great for guests. This is usually a soft introduction to our products, programs or community. The events are usually two to three hours long online or in person. We may even bring in outside trainers but the goal is to give value to our community. Some topics we've trained on are time management, wellness for busy moms, goal setting, etc.

11. **Weekly Team Calls**: These are always pretty similar: Announcements, recognition, mindset, skill set and call to action. Three to forty five minutes max. I think it's important to get the new people up there sharing their story. A testimonial (not a "trainamonial") one to two minutes max sharing their story, not a ten minute preaching session. These can get carried away so coach accordingly!

12. **Daily Team Trainings Monday through Friday**: The basics, mindset, skillset, social media, etc. This also trains the trainers! Most of my six-figure earners do these calls and rotate. I encourage them to bring up their new people on the calls as well so they are feeling seen and valued.

Phew! I hope that gives you a few ideas to incorporate.

Just know that these events we run are not always every year. We have always done our big team event and then we chose another event like a leadership bootcamp but the rest all determined the season and what the team needs and leaders want to execute.

Coach's Notes: Julia Thornhill's event-driven approach to network marketing is not just innovative; it's a comprehensive blueprint for achieving six figures and beyond. This strategy is centered around making an impact, fostering community, and enhancing the personal growth of team members. The span of events, from wealth summits to marriage retreats and charity events, showcases a deep commitment to not just business growth but personal and communal enrichment as well. Julia's focus on incorporating intention in every aspect, backed by her and Brandon's inspiring journey and investment in personal development, offers a model that's ripe for replication or adaptation according to your business's phase.

Whether you're directly implementing these strategies or envisioning them as part of your future growth, the essence lies in the transformation they promise—not just in business metrics but in personal lives and community well-being. This chapter offers invaluable insights into creating a culture that celebrates learning, achievement, and genuine connection, embodying what it truly means to lead with intention and purpose.

With that said, let's get straight into committees. This is one of my favorite ways to make your leaders feel valued and as if they have a voice and important role in the overall mission.

A committee is a collective of empowering individuals on your team, providing a voice, fostering a sense of purpose, and preventing burnout. It's a volunteer force, not a hired team, and certainly not a platform for mere complaints without solutions. This is a volunteer army, not a "you're hired" situation. It's also not the "complain with no solution" show. It's not the "I bring you the problems Jules and you you do it" show. It's the, "I'm in the trenches and have amazing ideas to enhance our mission" show.

Here are some tips:

1. It does not necessarily have to be a rank, although usually 50-100k sales a month is ideal.

2. Three to five people per committee. Too many cooks in the kitchen is exhausting.
3. Have them commit quarterly. This allows them to be replaced if they do not bring the value or show up at any given time.
4. Personally call them and invite them.
5. Have the committee vote on when to meet (once a week max, every two weeks is better).
6. Have a head of the committee member that runs it, you don't need to be micromanaging people. You didn't enroll to run an adult daycare center. You want to empower people with their God given gifts!

Here is how I currently run my organization top down:

CEO Council: The movers, the shakers, the innovators, the drivers, no more than three to five positions. Most of our six-figure earners are couples, so there will be more seasons, but these are my generals. These fluctuate every one to three years.

Communication Committee: They create all team challenges, documents, flyers, slide decks, boards, facebook groups, text chats and chats, etc. Usually working directly with my graphic designer.

Social Media Committee: You guessed it, social media. Tik tok and reels challenges, templates, ai prompts, etc.

Events Committee: From decor, to speaker flow to the whole vibe, they execute (I also usually bring in an event coordinator that works with the committee).

One-offs:

Gear Committee: t-shirts, swag, etc.
International Committees:
International committees (this is key when expanding globally). I believe that there are things in different markets that can only be seen by that country. Having a committee in place can help scale things

faster and get systems in place. You just need to make sure the person running them is trustworthy and educated enough to work with your designer. You don't want to reinvent the wheel here, you want to polish the wheel and maybe add a new rim if you know what I mean. It's easy to complicate and harder to simplify.

So that's it with committees. Think of them as a way to not wear all the hats but allow others to wear them. I think one of the hardest parts in leadership is wanting everything done perfectly. What I've learned over the years is to be okay with things being done 80% right. It's better than being done 100% and being burnt out. Learn to delegate not demand and learn to let go and let God.

Lastly, let's talk about the MISSION and VISION. I believe that you can create, craft and cultivate ANY community you want.

The bible says "without vision people perish". I believe it's the same for creating a community that lasts.

With that said, here's who I hire on salary, hourly or monthly to work with the committees and keep me sane with two little girls under three:

- **Project Manager**: Overseas all operations and Virtual Assistant
- **Virtual Assistant**: Pulls reports, creates chats, monitors FB groups, organizes calls, attends committee meetings, etc.
- **Graphic Designer**

Throughout my career I've started different movements. I've been successful in all of them but one. When I say "successful", I define that as: Successfully gathering hundreds and thousands of people coming together on zoom or at events for a common purpose and goal. I'm talking about bringing people together with actual integrity to change the world for good. Most of you are picking up what I'm putting down (you're my people). So you'll want to dial in your mission and vision.

Eight years ago my husband and I said we wanted to "create a community of faith-based couples we can trust our own children around". This was an internal vision I prayed on and it came true.

To date, my two-year old has been on forty-nine flights, seven countries, fourteen states and most of those trips were with our top earners and their kids. They were either paid for by the company, our events or because we just love each other and our kids are all best friends from around the world. Subsequently, almost all 100+ six-figure earners we've created have been couples.

My point of mentioning that is we were clear about a year in on what the community we wanted to create looked like. In the beginning, it was a crazy, wild learning experience that stretched our minds to what was capable for our life.

Overtime, we got really clear on who we wanted to work with and experience life with around the world.

So let's take some time now to figure out what that is for you. However, I want you to think about for a minute if you were direct to the company (and maybe you are) but imagine there was no upline support, no calls in place, nothing. Imagine from scratch right now that you could create a beautiful community. What does that community look like? What are their common problems, beliefs, fears, desires and dreams?

Your mission statement is the heartbeat "clearly articulating what your organization does and who it serves, embodying the essence of 'We do [X] for [Y].'"

Your vision statement is a glimpse into the future "envisioning the ideal future state and expressing what your organization aspires to become, encapsulating the essence of 'We aspire to be [X] in [Y].'"

So take a moment and think about this.

My community today is very much bold in their faith. We take the faith over fear approach. Lead or be led. The "We trust our community, not the government" vibe, if you know what I mean. Homeschooling is skyrocketing for a reason and I'm so here for it.

With that said, I should mention that it has evolved over the last eight years and in my opinion, I think reinventing your team, just like your own personal brand, is a good thing.

So, for example, one of our mission statements has been this: *We are "Unmasking the truth about Mental Wellness and Financial Fulfillment"*

Vision: *to create a million healthy, wealthy, happy homes.*

Boom. No fluff. No confusion. You know what you get. Most of our banners at our events have "FAITH. FAMILY. FREEDOM" on them because that's what WE believe that's how it should be - in that order.

Is everyone in our community obsessed with it? No. But the majority are, and that's okay if not everyone isn't. You can have sub-cultures in your team which I also believe is powerful.

Aim to empower your community over blowing up your own ego. It shouldn't be the YOU show. This is about the PEOPLE. It's about showing others what's possible.

If you've stayed with me on this journey, you're ready to wield the pen, script your story, and build a community that harmonizes with your soul. I bet you have what it takes. You have one of two things; that burning desire to change the world or the desire to be a part of something powerful.

Perhaps for the first time you're realizing that YOU get to choose. That YOU get to pick up the pen and write your own story. That YOU get to create ANY community you want, and I believe you can too. Just remember, lead with love, intention, integrity and purpose and sometimes you just need to let go and let God.

Xoxo,
Your friend,
Jules Aka Julia Thornhill: wife, mother, fierce friend and God-fearing proud network marketer.

Coach's Notes: Julia Thornhill's story is a powerful example of leading with intention in network marketing. By centering her approach on faith, family, and freedom, she and her husband have cultivated a community that not only excels in business but also in personal growth and shared values. Their focus on creating meaningful events and nurturing specific areas of life is a strategic blueprint for anyone looking to build a cohesive and motivated team.

For effective leadership, clearly define what your community stands for and weave these principles into all your actions and events. This method builds more than just a business; it fosters a network where every member can flourish. True leadership is about empowering your team and providing a platform for shared victories. Keep your vision and integrity at the forefront of your efforts, and watch as your community strengthens and expands.

"Success is the sum of small efforts,

repeated day in and day out."

— Robert Collier

BRI RICHARDSON

- Inaugural member of the Million Dollar Earner Hall of Fame, celebrating exceptional earnings and leadership.

- Renowned speaker who has graced the stages of prestigious industry events such as Go Pro and ANMP.

- Built an organization of over 600,000 distributors.

- Has built a reputation as a dynamic leader who leads from the front and inspires others to achieve their best.

- Respected for a no-excuse approach to business and a passionate heart that motivates others.

Success-One Day at a Time

Welcome to what very well could be the turning point in your entrepreneurial journey. I'm Bri Richardson, and I'm going to start by sharing with you a slice of my life that sparked a transformation not just in my career, but in my entire outlook on success and what it means to truly live life to the fullest. Don't worry, I'll also get down to the nuts and bolts of how it's done.

Twelve years ago at the age of 27, I found myself at a pivotal crossroad. I was out of a job, pregnant with my first child, and facing a decision that would redefine my future. At this time I narrowed down my options on how to proceed. Option one was the traditional route: Polish my resume, dive into the relentless world of job interviews, and hope for the best. Option two was a path less traveled, but one that resonated with my deepest desires—to earn at least $1,000 from home, allowing me the precious opportunity to be a stay at home mom.

My previous encounter with the network marketing industry at eighteen had been less than stellar, to put it mildly. I had failed, and in the echoes of my mother's words, I could hear the stinging label of "pyramid scheme" that so many had hastily attached to this misunderstood business model. But as fate would have it, a mindless act of scrolling through social media opened my eyes to a world of possibility. A product piqued my interest, and upon inquiring, I discovered the opportunity that lay beyond it.

The industry had evolved. Gone were the days of mandatory inventory stockpiles, the pressure of hosting parties in strangers' homes, and the cumbersome process of handling payments and deliveries. What lay before me was an opportunity akin to owning a modern-day franchise, but with an incredibly low cost of entry.

I was sold. My eyes were wide open to the potential that network marketing now held—a potential that was accessible, empowering, and aligned with the digital age. This was my chance to rewrite my story, to build a life of freedom and success on my own terms and that I did. By the age of twenty nine I had built a multi-million dollar business and "retired" my husband from the corporate world. I was speaking on big stages; not just my company stages but BIG ONES like *GoPro, The Most Powerful Women in Network Marketing* and training many colleagues at the *Association of Network Marketing Professionals*. There were articles written and my dream life was coming into complete focus.

What I realize today that I didn't back then was at that crossroads of my career, my decision to go all in with Network Marketing not only changed my life forever but it quite literally changed the trajectory of the legacy that I will leave my family with forever. Now I'm here to share with you the daily practices that have paved my way to success, and how you too can embark on this sweet journey of success, one day at a time.

To begin, mindset isn't just a piece of the puzzle; it's the very framework that holds every piece in place. As a top earner in the network marketing industry, I can tell you that success isn't a door you stumble upon by chance—it's one that requires the right keys to open. One of those keys, perhaps the most crucial, is mindset.

We are all wired differently, with unique predispositions and inclinations. Some of us are natural self-starters, driven by the sheer thrill of success. For others, the journey requires a more disciplined approach, a conscious effort to rewire our mindset to align with our aspirations. This is where the philosophy of "one day at a time" becomes not just a mantra, but a method.

Yes, having goals and a clear vision is essential. It's challenging to reach a destination when you're unsure of its location. But the true magic happens when we distill our grand ambitions into manageable, bite-sized pieces—when we break down the monumental goal into daily action steps. The objective is simple yet profound: Collect Success.

Imagine treating each day as a self-contained opportunity for triumph, as if there were no tomorrow to depend on or worry about. This is the day that matters—the only day you need to focus on to inch closer to your ultimate success. By adopting this mindset, you create a powerful ripple effect, where each day that you complete your daily method of operation (DMO) is a step closer to the life you envision. Each day completed is one success collected.

Think about the power of consistent action, no matter how small. It's about creating a chain of successes, one day at a time as it forms a chain and it's this chain that will eventually bear the weight of your dreams. The beauty of this approach is that it's accessible to everyone. Whether you're a seasoned entrepreneur or just starting, the principle remains the same: Consistent, daily actions lead to significant results.

To cultivate this mindset, start by defining your big goal. Then, reverse-engineer it into what needs to be accomplished each day. These aren't just tasks, they're your stepping stones to success. Each completed action is a victory, a reason to celebrate, and a building block for tomorrow's achievements.

But how do you stay disciplined enough to "collect success" each day? It begins with a commitment to yourself. It's a promise that today's actions are non-negotiable, that they are as vital as breathing. It's about understanding that discipline is not a punishment but a pathway to freedom—the freedom to live the life you've always wanted.

Remember, the mind is like a muscle, and just like any muscle, it can be trained and strengthened. Start by feeding it positive affirmations, surround yourself with motivational influences, and immerse yourself in environments that foster growth. Reflect on and celebrate your successes, no matter how small, and let them fuel your journey.

As you read this, know that the power to change your life lies within you, in the mindset you choose to adopt. Recognize the word *choose* in that last sentence. It's a journey I delve deeper into in my book *Legacy Success*, where I explore the intricacies of mindset and the actionable steps to transform your daily habits into a legacy of success.

So, as you turn the pages of this chapter, ask yourself: Are you ready to "collect success"? Are you prepared to take the steps necessary to rewire your mindset and unlock the doors to your dreams? Because when you do, that's when the real transformation begins—one day at a time.

In the world of network marketing, your Daily Method of Operation (DMO) is the engine that powers your journey to success. It's the daily habits and actions that, when consistently applied, can lead to the creation of a multimillion-dollar business. I've lived this truth, having built two such businesses myself, and I'm excited to share with you the six-step formula that was the backbone of my building to this success.

Coach's Notes: Bri Richardson's story is a perfect example of the power of daily dedication and the strategic approach to success. As someone who has transformed her life through network marketing, Bri's insights are invaluable. Her focus on breaking down lofty goals into daily actionable steps underscores a fundamental truth in both life and business: Consistency is key.

Adopting a "one day at a time" mindset isn't just motivational advice; it's a practical strategy for sustainable success. Bri's six-step formula for

Daily Method of Operation (DMO) demonstrates how regular, focused actions can compound over time, leading to significant achievements. This approach aligns perfectly with the concept of "collecting success," where every day counts as a victory towards the bigger picture.

Bri's is one of the very top earners in network marketing. Her story and strategies serve as a blueprint for anyone aiming to achieve not just in network marketing but in any endeavor that requires perseverance and a positive outlook. Implementing her daily practices can pave your way to success, reinforcing the idea that with the right mindset and commitment, anyone can transform their dreams into reality. Remember, success is a series of small wins, and with dedication, those wins can lead to monumental achievements.

Step 1: Make New Contacts

The first step is foundational: Make new contacts. Network marketing is, at its core, a relationship business. It's about expanding your circle, making new friends, and nurturing those connections. While the digital age tempts us to measure our worth in likes and comments, the real currency of our industry is the personal connections we forge with our network.

Each day, ask yourself, "Who will I reach out to today that I haven't connected with about my business or product?" This question isn't just about ticking a box. It's about genuinely engaging with others and showing interest in their lives. The second question to ponder is, "how many new people am I reaching out to?" The answer to this will dictate the pace of your progress. The more people you connect with, the faster you'll move towards your goals.

To be completely transparent, in the beginning, this was the scariest part of the whole process and shoot, it was step one! You can't move on if you don't do step one! So, there were many days where I would open the message on Facebook Messenger, cultivate my approach, close my eyes or turn my head away from the screen and just hit enter. I was terrified! The only thing that broke that mindset block for me was doing it over and over and over and...you get the picture. Think of it as a math equation, the more you send the more positive responses you get and THAT is what built my confidence to finally open my eyes. So, no matter how you have to do it, just start doing it.

Step 2: Make a Sale

The second step in your DMO isn't about the pressure of closing a sale every single day; it's about taking deliberate actions that will eventually lead to sales. It's the understanding that each effort you make today plants the seeds for future harvests. So, the pivotal question is, what can you do today to introduce someone to your products?

Consider the myriad of ways you can showcase your offerings. Social media content is a powerful tool; it's your virtual storefront. Craft posts that educate, inspire, and demonstrate the value of what you're offering. Remember, it's not just about the product itself, but the story and lifestyle it represents. It's about what problem you can solve and who it can help.

In-person interactions are equally valuable. Tastings, samplings, and live demonstrations allow people to experience the benefits firsthand, creating a memorable impression that can lead to a sale. These experiences bridge the gap between curiosity and commitment.

Every action, whether it's a post, a sample, or a conversation, is a step towards a sale. It's about consistent, value-driven exposure. By putting new people in front of your products daily, you're not just hoping for sales; you're actively cultivating them. Keep your focus on the actions that lead to sales, and trust that with persistence and passion, the results will follow.

Coach's Notes: Bri nails it with her approach to making sales a part of your daily activities without the pressure. It's about understanding the importance of consistent, value-driven actions that lead to sales. The key here is to focus on solving problems and helping others through your products. Utilize every tool at your disposal, from social media to in-person interactions, to showcase the value and lifestyle your products offer.

Remember, every action you take is planting seeds for future sales. Keep at it, stay passionate, and the sales will come. This strategy isn't just about making sales; it's about building trust and creating lasting relationships with your customers.

Step 3: Follow Up

The third step of your DMO is where the magic happens: Follow up. This step is crucial and often where many network marketers miss the mark. The fortune, as they say, is in the follow-up. It's about nurturing relationships, showing genuine interest, and providing value consistently.

Following up can take many forms. It could be checking in with a current customer to ensure they're delighted with their product experience. It's an opportunity to answer questions, offer tips, or even suggest complementary products that could enhance their satisfaction.

For prospects who've shown interest but haven't made a purchase, a follow-up is your chance to reignite that spark. Remind them of the benefits they were excited about and address any hesitations they may have. Your persistence and attention could be the nudge they need to take the leap.

Don't forget those who've expressed interest in the business side of things. A follow-up with them could mean expanding your team and multiplying your success. It's about maintaining that connection and demonstrating the support and opportunities that await them.

In every case, your follow-up should be personal, timely, and tailored to the individual. It's not just about making a sale or growing your team; it's about building trust and establishing long-term relationships. Remember, in network marketing, you're not closing a sale; you're opening a relationship.

Step 4: Offer the Opportunity

Step four is where you lay the groundwork for long-term financial freedom. It's the step that separates the short-sighted from the visionaries. Remember, only broke people work solely for today's pay. Rich people play the long game, focusing on future gains. This step is all about offering the opportunity.

Let me share a quick story to illustrate the cadence of these steps to success. When I was first building my business, I followed this exact sequence. I reached out to a multitude of people, actively shared and promoted my products, and made a boatload of sales. But I didn't stop there. I diligently followed up with every single customer, inquiring about their product experience and what they loved about it. Then, I simply offered each one the opportunity to promote the product alongside me and earn some extra cash.

This approach wasn't just about selling products; it was about building a community, a network of distributors who shared the vision and passion for the products. By offering the opportunity, I was inviting them to be a part of something bigger, to join a journey towards financial independence and personal growth.

The results speak for themselves. Over the span of seven years, this methodical approach helped me build an organization of over 600,000 distributors. It's a testament to the power of the process. Trust in it, embrace it, and watch as it works wonders for you, too. The more you offer the opportunity, the more you'll see your efforts compound into the kind of wealth that lasts.

Keep in mind, you can also lead with the opportunity, it doesn't have to come on the back end of a sale. In fact, today, I offer the opportunity to build with me at two touch points. First when they are ready to order and have asked for a link and next once they have had a product experience and are a raving fan.

Step 5: Personal Development

The fifth and final step of your DMO is personal development, an essential ingredient in your daily routine. Remember, if you're not growing, you're slowing. Personal growth is the fuel that propels you forward in your business and in life. One of my biggest mentors, Eric Worre, emphasizes the importance of mastering the seven skills of network marketing. Choose one skill and dedicate yourself to becoming a master at it. Once you've achieved that, move on to the next.

Personal development can come from various sources – a book that challenges your thinking, a blog that offers fresh strategies, a YouTube video that motivates, a podcast that expands your knowledge, or a team training that hones your craft. Make a commitment to plug into some form of personal development every single day. It's not just about the information you consume; it's about the transformation that occurs within you as you apply what you learn.

By consistently investing in your personal growth, you'll not only become a more effective network marketer but also a more well-rounded and resilient individual and eventually a teacher. So, pick a skill, train diligently, and watch as your confidence grows you into a leader of leaders where you walk a little taller, sit up a little straighter and talk a little more proud.

Step 6: Team Touch

Step six comes into play as soon as you personally sponsor one person. As you begin to build your team, "Team Touch" becomes a pivotal part of your DMO. It's all about reaching out and encouraging your team members. This step is about connection and support, which can manifest in various ways. It could be a simple message to check in on how they're doing, asking if they need help with their business, or even sharing a quick motivational quote to uplift their spirits.

As you grow more confident in leadership, consider hosting a brief fifteen minute team training or presentation to foster a sense of community and shared learning. These moments are invaluable for team cohesion and can spark inspiration and action. Remember, your team's success is your success, so make it a point to touch base with them regularly. A little encouragement goes a long way in building a strong, motivated, and successful team.

To close us out, let's circle back to the essence of these six steps—they are your blueprint for crafting a robust Daily Method of Operation (DMO), with an emphasis on "daily." The key to accumulating your successes, one day at a time, is to commit to each step, every single day. To ensure consistency and focus, make it a habit to create your DMO list each night before you close your eyes. The more specific you are with your tasks, the more productive and purposeful your days will become.

Don't just plan to reach out to a certain number of new people. Identify exactly WHO you will contact. Detail the content you intend to create or share. Schedule that coffee meet-up to chat about products, and pinpoint whose problems you're going to solve. The follow-up is where many drop the ball, and I believe it's where half, if not more, of potential business is lost due to inconsistency. Make it your mission to never let that crucial step slip through the cracks.

In my experience, a significant portion of my time is well-spent in step four, offering the opportunity to everyone I encounter. This opportunity isn't just for those in need, it's for anyone with a passion to make an impact. While personal growth is vital, avoid becoming a perpetual student. Apply what you learn, take action, and start building the community and business you've always dreamed of and the life you deserve.

Remember, your DMO isn't just a to-do list; it's a commitment to your future, a daily contract with yourself to push forward, to innovate, and to connect. By following these steps, you're not just working towards financial freedom; you're cultivating a lifestyle that resonates with your deepest values and aspirations. So, take these words, your passion, and your drive, and go out there to create the life you deserve. Practice developing an unshakable, consistent and disciplined mindset that will lead you to success, one day at a time.

Coach's Notes: The six steps Bri Richardson outlines serve as a vital blueprint for establishing a successful Daily Method of Operation (DMO). Emphasizing daily commitment, these steps transform routine tasks into strategic actions towards success. Crafting your DMO list nightly sharpens focus and boosts productivity, ensuring every action is intentional and aligned with your goals.

The essence lies in not just planning but executing with precision—knowing who to contact, what content to share, and addressing specific needs. Consistent follow-up is crucial; it's often where opportunities are won or lost.

This method is more than a roadmap to financial freedom; it's a blueprint for a fulfilling lifestyle, underpinned by a disciplined mindset. Embrace these daily commitments to innovate, connect, and gradually build the dream life and business you envision.

"I do what others Won't so I can experience things others Don't!"

— Burke Green

BURKE GREEN

- Boasts over three decades of unparalleled success and leadership in the Network Marketing industry, achieving the highest pin level in three separate companies.

- As a founding distributor of two prosperous ventures, Burke has played a pivotal role in their ascent to success, cultivating organizations with over 1 million distributors.

- Burke's organizations have generated over $20 billion in sales and more than a billion dollars in commissions, showcasing his knack for fostering thriving business ecosystems globally, spanning 60 countries.

- Recognized as one of the industry's most sought-after trainers, Burke's innovative (How To) training system reflects his dedication to equipping distributors with skills for success.

- Beyond leadership and training, Burke is an authority on compensation plans, leveraging over three decades of experience to optimize earnings for himself and his teams.

Mastering The Game You Are Playing

Coach's Notes: Burke Green's journey from a farm in Wyoming to becoming a sage in the network marketing industry underscores a vital lesson: Understanding the game you're playing is crucial. His basketball anecdote isn't just a humorous tale; it's a powerful metaphor for the importance of knowing the rules of your chosen field. In network marketing, this translates to grasping the nuances of the compensation model and the industry's dynamics. Burke's insights highlight the criticality of preparation, research, and commitment in succeeding in network marketing. His story and subsequent success serve as an invaluable blueprint for those aspiring to make their mark in this competitive landscape. Pay attention to Burke's wisdom—his experience and understanding of the game's "rules" offer a roadmap to mastering network marketing.

To win in any game, it's crucial to understand the rules. If you're reading this book or immersing yourself in this industry, and particularly if you're associated with Rob Sperry, I feel that it is safe to make a couple of assumptions. First, it's likely that you are curious about network marketing as a career, or at the very least you aspire to generate substantial income - transforming it into a viable side hustle. I would like to share with you a few things that I have learned about the network marketing game from many years of experience in this industry. To truly thrive and be a real player, you must understand the rules of the game you're playing. Before we dive in, I would like to share a story with you.

My name is Burke Green. I grew up on a farm in Alta, Wyoming, which is a little rural community on the western side of the Tetons from Jackson Hole. There were thirty of us kids in my grade school. That's grades one through six, and we didn't have organized sports. After grade school, I went to middle school in Driggs, Idaho. This was before the NBA youth programs such as Junior Jazz were really big. I had a lot of experience playing basketball on the playground and I loved all sports. I especially loved contact sports like football. I was a pretty big kid for my age and was also pretty athletic, so I tried out for the basketball team in seventh grade. The time came for our very first game. I was excited to play! I wasn't a starter in the game, but for some reason, the coach decided to throw me into the mix. This is where it gets good.

When the coach put me in the game, I ran down the court to set up the defense. As I previously shared, I was pretty big for my age and, growing up with big brothers, I was kind of the rough and tumble type. As I stood under the basket, the point guard from the other team came down the court, and drove the middle lane towards me. I had just finished the football season playing middle linebacker when I started basketball. When he came driving in at full speed I thought, there's no way this little dude is going to score on me.

I basically went up with my full body and blocked him as he tried to make a shot! In the process of blocking him, I knocked him down. For reasons that are obvious to me now, but weren't then, the shooting foul was called on me. This was the first play of my basketball career. Everybody lined up on the foul line while the opposing player was setting up to shoot. Just before he shot the ball I heard the coach yell "Burke, get the ball." So I thought, Okay, let's go. Well, he missed the first shot and the ball bounced off the rim to the other side of the court. I can't exactly remember how it happened, but I ended up with the ball and there were several opposing team members laying on the ground. The whistle blew and guess what? I got called for another foul. Now we were in the penalty so it was a one and one situation on the foul shots.

Again we lined up. I got ready. They shot the ball. They missed the ball and I got the rebound again. If I'm anything, I'm consistent. Again there were players from the opposing team on the ground. At this point I was very confused as to why the ref kept calling fouls on me. I got the ball, wasn't that the goal? This same scenario happened four times in a row. Opposing team would shoot the foul shot, he would miss, I got the rebound and a couple of people ended up on the floor. My very first organized game of basketball ended up with me fouling out of the game with five fouls in less than one minute of play. After that first foul, the opposing team never left the foul line until I fouled out.

I came off the court confused and pretty frustrated. I felt that I had done what was asked of me. I got the ball. I expressed this to my coach who was chuckling as I came over to him.

Coach said, "Burke, sit down. We've got to have a talk about what was happening. I love the effort and enthusiasm, but you need to learn the rules of the game."

I didn't understand the rules of the game that I was playing. I was playing football on the basketball court, and because I didn't understand the rules, I was penalized and basically taken out of the game very quickly. In less than one minute, I received five fouls and had to sit on the bench for the rest of the game. That is how my basketball career started.

What does that story have to do with our industry? I'd like to make some comparisons. I was taught and I think many of us were, that we should go to high school to get good grades, so we can go to college. We then go to college to get good grades to get a good job. When we do all that, then we do the research, preparation and we go through the process of getting a job. We do all the different things. Then when we sit down. In our first job interview, we went through the process. Our boss gives us the definition of the job description. We go to work and we negotiate our salary, then we go to work.

We do all those things! Well, in this industry, in the direct sales industry, the network marketing industry, typically a friend calls us, or we answer a Facebook post or something like that. Then we join the business. We enter this industry with the mindset of trying it for ninety days and see how it goes, and if we're not making X amount of money or if the product isn't exactly what we think it should be, we move on to the next company. Even though we have not given it the time to grow or the effort to make it happen we move on. What would happen if we did that in our careers?

Now, here's the thing that's crazy to me. When I see people do this, and I've been doing this for thirty three years, it absolutely astounds me how people enter this business and they say, "Oh, my gosh! I joined this business, I joined this industry, and I am going to get rich!" With no forethought, with no thinking about it, with no study, no research, none of those things.

I have a couple of questions that I want to ask you, and I want you to think about this now. I travel all over the world doing trainings, meetings, doing those sorts of things, and I always ask these two questions:

The first question, and I want you to think about this is, how many of you before today have been involved, exposed, or seen another network marketing company or direct sales company?

When I ask that question, it doesn't matter where in the world I am. At this point every single hand goes up. At this point in the world everyone has been exposed or involved in this industry.

When I ask the next question, and that is how many of you had a good experience or actually made money with your previous company? Guess what happens? Probably less than 10% of the hands go up now. The crazy part about that is as I go around and I'm talking to people, I talk to them about the compensation model. That's basically what we're going to be talking about today is understanding the game and rules and game that you're playing. That's the compensation model. How do we get paid? Okay, we don't just sign up and all of a sudden money starts rolling in. This is a very competitive industry at this point. Just like in any industry, those that are the talented and the most educated usually have a better shot at winning. But, understanding the rules of the game is essential.

There are essentially five different compensation models:

1. There's a stair step breakaway

2. There's a matrix

3. There's unilevel and binary

4. Then there's a hybrid binary compensation model

5. Hybrid compensation model

Now, when people talk about those different models. That is literally how we get paid in this industry. When we sell a product, there's a commission derived, and that's how we are paid. Well again, let me ask a question. Do you know the nuances of each one of these compensation models? Do you know how to maximize or get the most commissions possible out of each one of these compensation models, or do you just join a company? Hope and for the best, and I've even heard top distributors of companies go. For some, they don't really understand how the compensation plan works. They just want to work and the checks just started rolling in. They just signed up and, gosh, I did this, and money started coming in. Well, guys, that's ridiculous. If you're looking at creating a long-term residual income. You need to understand the game that you're playing.

If you don't, you will be like me in my basketball game, where you will be disappointed and out of the game, or you will be penalized before you even get started, and it'll be very short lived, and then it won't be a good experience, and you'll move on to the next company. Over and over again. Do you know the nuances of their compensation model that would lead you to the next level of income?

When you make a decision to join a company. Is that a product based decision? Is that a compensation model-based decision? Or is it just your friend joins? So you're going to join them, and it's gonna be a fun ride.

If you're looking to create income with this industry, you need to become better at getting involved in the compensation model. Each model has its own nuances. Each model has its good, bad, and ugly. But the biggest thing that I see in this industry is that the vast majority of people don't have any idea, really, how the compensation model works. They don't have any idea how the compensation model actually pays out, how it calculates commissions and how the best way to maximize those commissions are.

Coach's Notes: Burke Green's basketball story underscores a key lesson for network marketing: The importance of understanding your company's compensation plan. Just like knowing the rules of basketball prevents fouls, understanding the nuances of your compensation model is essential for success. Whether it's a stair-step, matrix, unilevel, binary, or hybrid, each plan has its unique advantages and strategies for maximizing earnings. Burke emphasizes that success isn't about luck but about informed, strategic action. This insight is crucial for anyone serious about making a significant income in network marketing.

So here's my suggestion: When you get involved in a company, you need to understand and do the research necessary to make a smart decision for your future. You need to study. You need to read books. You need to talk to mentors who are doing what you want to do. If you want to make $5,000 a month. Talk to somebody making $5,000 a month. If you want to make $10,000 a month, talk to someone making $10,000 a month. If you want to make $100,000 a month, talk to someone making $100,000 a month. It doesn't matter really what the number is, because this industry will allow you to create any income that you want. But one thing you need to understand is you need to grow as an individual to that level of income just because you joined a company and you joined the network marketing industry that does not give you the God-given right to make $10,000 a month. What are people doing today to make $10,000 a month in this industry? They have studied and learned and grown into that person that is qualified to make that sort of income.

You know this is a competitive industry. When you talk to someone. Do you know the difference between a stair step breakaway and a unilevel and a matrix and a binary? Can you tell them the difference? Or are you just hoping for the best, you? Oh, we got this cool, cool product.

Guess what?

Every company has a cool product. Every company has a viable product, that if people use it, take it, do whatever they need to do with it, they probably derive benefit. In my opinion. The compensation model is one of the biggest issues that people overlook when trying to create an income and trying to create a career in this industry. So if you don't know what your compensation model is or how it works or you're not quite sure-you don't know the rules of the game.

Do you have a strategy to maximize the compensation plan? When I sign someone up I have 3 goals :

1. I want to get them on the product for the benefits they're going to receive.

2. I want to help them make enough money to get their products paid for.

3. I want to move them into profitability.

Do you know how to do that? Do you know what the break-even point is in your compensation model? You know, if people are on a $150 or a $250 a month auto ship. What is it going to take to make $150 to $250 dollars a month? How many people do you have to recruit? How many people have to be on an auto ship? Do you know the numbers?

The next step? Do you know the numbers to help move them into profitability? Do you know what it takes to actually rank up and do the volume? If you don't do that, you're fooling yourselves as far as going out and creating a career in this industry.

So here's my advice: When you look at a compensation model, you need to be able to understand how it pays out. Get with a competent and upline or competent person you know. I've done a lot of consulting around the industry. It's astounding to me how many executives of companies and how many owners of companies don't even know how the compensation models will work, other than, that is what some consultant told them it was a great model, and that sort of thing. They don't know the requirements that it takes. They don't know the different nuances of how their compensation plan works. Get with a confident upline or with a competent person who understands the industry, who understands the models and set up a strategy and a game plan to:

1. Get people to buy your product.

2. Help them get that product paid for.

3. Help you people move into profitability.

From that point on, once they're profitable. The next thing we need to do is help them replace their income from their current job or current career, so they can become a full time member of your team. So with that, hopefully, this has been helpful. See you at the top!

Coach's Notes: Burke's advice is important for anyone looking to master network marketing. It's all about understanding the game you're playing—knowing your compensation plan inside out. Just joining a company doesn't entitle anyone to earn big; it's about growing into the person who can. This means studying, learning from those already successful, and having a clear strategy. Burke outlines a brilliant approach: Get people loving your product, help them cover their costs, then guide them into making a profit. Knowing the nuances of your compensation model and having a plan to maximize it are key steps often overlooked. His emphasis on being informed, having a strategy for growth, and understanding how to navigate the compensation plan to achieve success is invaluable advice. This is the blueprint for turning aspirations into achievements in network marketing.

*"If you don't sow,
you don't reap...."*

— Jim Rohn

LANCE CONRAD

- Top recruiter out of a million distributors.

- 16 years industry experience.

- Built business in 40 plus countries.

- Helped 400+ people earn a six figure income over the last 3.5 years.

- Took a company from 0 to $100M in 13 months.

Everybody Hates Network Marketing, And It's All Your Fault

When I first got into network marketing, I was 33. A friend of mine called me up and said, "Hey, let's go do skincare." He was 27. Every 27 and 33-year-old wanted to sell facials, but he was brave enough and bold enough to make it big enough that I was interested. It ended up becoming a partnership, and it changed my life and sent me on a journey around the world where I've trained over a million people around the world. That was Rob Sperry, who had the guts to call me. That was extremely brave. I owned my own business. I had ten employees, and he was gutsy enough to call me. I was the first person he called. So, I want to talk about that. I jumped into that company, and there's nothing wrong with skincare. I love skincare. It's consumable, so people use it every month. Skincare companies are great companies, and now that I'm getting older here, I could use more skincare in my life. But at that point in time, it wasn't like I woke up that morning and said, "I'm going to go do facials."

Little did I know, this leap into skincare was just the beginning of an unexpected adventure. I jumped in, and the first four people I called said yes. I said, "I'm doing this. You're doing this. Give me your credit card. Say yes, we're doing it." It was a $1,600 buy-in for that deal. I thought I was off to the races. I hit the first rank. I made like 900 bucks in twelve hours. I'm like, "Oh my gosh, sell my business. Quit everything. I'm a full-time networker. This is going to be great." So then I called those four people up and said, "Okay, so who are your four people? When are we going to talk to your four people?" I got crickets. "Oh yeah, well, I'm busy. I'm at work. Call me later." So that was like at eight in the morning. So at nine thirty, I'd call them again. "Okay, who are we calling? Where are you for? When's our meetings?" Crickets, noon, eight. Crickets by three.

I'm like, "Shawnee, you're my sister. I know you speak English and I speak Spanish. Oh, sorry, you got to go," nad she'd hang up on me. Pretty soon those four people didn't want to talk to me anymore. Okay, so what happened? I recruited followers, I recruited customers. I recruited people into my business that didn't have that same level of commitment in my business as I did. I wanted to make millions of dollars with it. That's why I joined. Of course, that's why everybody else would join. Those people were not the right people to go build monster teams with. So I started recruiting customers. I started recruiting followers. I started to build a team, and then I had a training where, look, if you could bring five fantastic people into your business, five influential people into your business, five people that really are going to treat it like a business, it will make you millions of dollars. My fave five. Alright? I was recruiting the wrong people. I was talking to the wrong people. I was trying to find customers. I was trying to find followers. What I needed was leaders. This is the leadership business. if you find customers and you find followers and you are building a business that you are going to have to babysit for the rest of your life, but if you get true leadership into your business, you've created true leverage and it will take on a life of its own.

Realizing the need for a strategic pivot, I decided to take a more targeted approach. So, I went home and made a list. Now, I had some pretty good people on that list, and I thought, "Alright." I was a recruiter, a headhunter. Four of my best friends were recruiters or headhunters. They'd been good at recruiting people. "Man, I'll just put this team together." By the way, I'd made all of them a lot of money. They were really good friends. They'd made me money in some cases, but we'd been partners for a lot of years, and I figured, "Man, I'll get them in my business. I'll launch my business, and I'll be done. I can retire, right? It's just that easy, right?"

So, I called Casey, Mark, Chad, and Nadine. Now, these are good friends, not okay friends, business partners, longtime friends, who I made a lot of money for. All four of them said no. No, they didn't just say no. They said, "Heck no." No, it was worse than that. I couldn't even get them to come to meet with me, not to a meeting. But if it was a meeting about networking, they didn't want to come. One of them laughed at me. One of them said, "Really? Is it that hard for you right now? Do you need a loan?" Like they were worried about me, but all four of them just flat out shut me down.

What are you going to do, right? There's my wishlist, there's my chicken list, there's the guys that I was going to build and the lady that I was going to build my future around, but they're not the most influential people that I know. So, I put on my list this guy named John. Now, John had just become famous in our state. He had just sold his company for hundreds of millions of dollars. We're talking about a 30-year-old, somebody in his mid-thirties that's worth over a hundred million dollars, like liquid cash money done. He's got every car in the garage you could possibly want. I actually told him when I went to his garage that he had all the posters that I had growing up, and he's like, "I know nothing about cars. That's what I did. I went out and bought all the posters," so Lambo, Ferrari, Porsche, all that.

So I went and pitched John why he should join my business with me and how it would change people's lives and how it would be the most fulfilling thing he ever did. Guess what? He shut me down. Okay, so what did I learn? Well, I learned that after I had those conversations, talking to anybody else became so easy. I had just got shut down majorly by my biggest chicken list, my biggest people. But talking to an average person at this point, I was like, "Oh, okay. What's the worst they can say?" It was no, and I'm still friends with all those people. So the world didn't end. It didn't stop turning, and now it made it easier to talk to other people. The other thing that did is it changed my expectations of who I was looking for and who to work with. So I was recruiting, building, going until I found this guy named Robert. Robert was young and he was just crazy enough to talk to anyone. He put me on with a guy through somebody he knew and somebody they knew. He put me on with a lady named Diane. Diane Cottle was a really successful realtor. All of a sudden, I found a leader, a partner, somebody I could run with, and I hit a rank and it was about 25,000 to 30,000 of volume with that lady in her first month, which is about what I did in my first month, which made about a $10,000 check.

Coach's Notes: Lance Conrad's path in network marketing emphasizes the power of daring to act and the strategic choice of recruits. Jumping into the industry at 33, after a call from me, he began his network marketing journey, quickly learning the importance of selecting leaders rather than finding anyone interested.

I learned more from Lance than any other leader in network marketing. I lacked confidence and boldness but borrowed from him until I had my own. As a close friend who introduced him to network marketing, I've observed Lance's development into a significant figure in the network marketing profession. Most network marketers go for what we call the low hanging fruit. Those who will for sure say yes. Lance shows the opposite is not just possible but is another way for many to have success.

Suddenly, we had a story, and I had someone who was moving as fast as I was, treating it as a business just like me, and my business began to change. We attracted other leaders. She brought in a lady named Tiffany. Tiffany went and hit about a 25,000 to 30,000 volume rank, which made her about seven to eight thousand dollars. Then the next month, we did it with someone else. Then the next, all of a sudden, we were attracting leader after leader, influencer after influencer because we were setting that expectation. When we talked to these people, it was a different kind of conversation. It wasn't about this little networking thing; it was big. We were talking about market share, about cities, states, countries. We discussed how to grow a business starting from a local market, then expanding into another local or nearby market, and then growing to other states. From there, we were taken across the country, and suddenly we were talking about distribution, market channels, partnerships, strategic partnerships. You'll notice the language I'm using is not typical network marketing language. I'm talking to influential people. These were not professional network marketers. So, I wasn't using network marketing speak. I wasn't talking CV, PV, TV— don't do TV it just crushes your business, right? I was talking about strategic partnerships, about market shares, about cities, states, countries. If you could really do well in your city, you could make hundreds, if not thousands, of dollars. If you could do well in your state, you could make thousands of dollars. If you could do well across the country, you could make tens of thousands of dollars a month. If you could do well internationally, you could make a hundred thousand dollars or more in monthly income. We were looking for strategic partners. You're probably thinking, "Oh, but I'm not you, and I can't talk like that, and I don't have that credibility." Knock it off; stop making yourself the issue, right?

So here's the point. It's not about you. It's about your company. You're in a great company, or you wouldn't be there. It's about your product. What's your company's history? What's your company's total sales? What attracted you to that company? What's the product? What is the new product, the hot product, the sexy product? What's the product that people are getting excited about? So, you stop making it about yourself; make it about someone else. That way, if they reject it, they're not rejecting you; they're rejecting a company or a product. Make it about your upline, but don't say upline; say your strategic partner. So, you have an opportunity to put the right people in front of the right partnership, right? If you do that, see, now you are making it big. I always made network marketing really big. I said, "I need to meet with you today or tomorrow. Next week never comes, and next month, forget about it." They're going to have ten other excuses that come in the middle between now and next week. So, if you don't make it today and you don't make it tomorrow, just forget about it. It's never going to happen. If it's so big that it's going to be life-changing, if it's that kind of opportunity, you want them to make time in their schedule, not try to fit you in the cracks of their schedule. I've shown up on people's doorsteps at 10:30 at night that I barely knew or didn't know referrals to have a meeting because that's when they were available. I would tell them, "Look, I'm going to make millions of dollars with this business. I'm looking for partners that want to go to the top with me." You know what they'd tell me? "I believe you because you're here at my house at 10:30 at night." So, if you make it big, they'll treat it big. If you make it small, they'll treat it small. So here's the list. I'm going to give you some lists, some takeaways, a challenge, and I'm running out of time. I could just tell stories for hours. So, oh, one last story. I got better at bringing in influencers from there; I've brought in the right influencers and been able to build teams of 10,000 plus people. One of my last big blitzes, I did that in less than a month.

We did $972,000 of volume with no pre-launch with one right influential person, but really, a leader is worth more than thousands of followers. I would trade whole teams of people to be able to partner up with the right people. If you change your mindset and your expectations, you're going to realize that leaders attract market share. They attract followers; they attract everything else that you want within your business, and finding the right leader is worth the chase because it will change your business and it will change your life.

So, who do you want in your business? You want people that are already influential, that already have circles of influence and have credibility within those circles of influence. So, write this down. You want anybody that's made six figures annually in any walk of life; put them on your wishlist. Fitness professionals, teachers, coaches, pastors, priests, professional MLMers that have made over $5,000 a month—these are the people I'd put on my list. I'd go make a list. Your fave five, the five people that you most want in your business. Write them down. This is your chicken list. Guess what? We're going to dust it off. Now, here's the great thing about it. There are two questions everybody asks themselves: Can I do it? Is it worth it? These people already know they can do it.

So, you've just got to show them that it's worth it. The timing's right, the product's right, the partnership's right. You've just got to show them part of it. The other thing about it, they don't get hit as often. If it's your chicken list, it's everybody else's chicken list. They're not getting hit up nearly as often as you might think, and they're going to look at it with more fresh eyes than you think. The next thing I would tell you, get other people involved, especially if you don't have a check, if you don't have a ranking. Then your goal is to sell the appointment. I need you to meet my friend who's made millions of dollars in this industry. I need you to meet this executive at this company that helps partner with me and helps us create market share. Because I believe you could do this in the seven-figure annual type income, which the top leaders in this company, that's what they make.

We're looking for strategic partners to open up the Western states, the Eastern states, to open up South America. You need to make it big. You need to make it bold. You need to be confident about it. Don't make it small. If you're going to bring on a partner to do a three-way call, I guarantee you that they're willing to do it for your chicken list, for your best people, just about anybody is willing to talk to them. If you've already addressed what your company is, what it sells, and that you've already made them the big kahuna, that they're the person you want to partner with, that they're the ones that have made millions of dollars. So, if you prep it so that by the time they do the three-way call, it's not a cold call.

I don't care who it is, anybody in your upline will do it, but don't put them on a cold call. You'll waste their time, you'll waste your credibility, and you'll never get a three-way call with that person again. So, sell the appointment, make it really big, make the pitch really short, and then sell the appointment. Don't make yourself the issue. Make your company the issue, the product the issue, the timing the issue, and the ability to work with the strategic partner. Make that the issue. Here is the challenge; I want you to call five people on your chicken list over the next twenty four hours. You need to do it now. You need to get courage. You need to get brave, all with the goal of just getting them to look at the opportunity. That's your job, not to sell them, not to close them.

Make it big enough that they go see it. I'm working with somebody that's made X number of millions of dollars in this business, and you need to meet them. I believe you have more skills than even they do. If I partner you up, there's no telling what you could do. We've got the hottest product in the marketplace right now, and the timing's fantastic. If you meet this person and get trained by this person, there's no stopping you. See, you notice it wasn't about me. It wasn't about partnering with me; it was about the company, it was about the product, it was about the partnership. So, I'm going to give you a good, better, best challenge.

Good is to reach out to five people on your chicken list in the next twenty four hours. That's good because it took some bravery, and you might get shot down just like I did. All my first five people all shot me down, but it raised my expectations and made all my other calls easier.

Better would be to get in front of or get on a real pitch. Hey, I reach out to them, that's good. If I could really make a presentation and really make a pitch to them, that's better. I would keep it really short, three minutes or less with the call to action or get on the next webinar or get to the next meeting. But if you really make a presentation with a call to action to five of your influential people, just like pat yourself on the back, that's better.

Best is to do a three-way call or any type of three way validation with an upline mentor, or to do a face-to-face presentation, ideally with an upline mentor that could bring credibility, that could bring PACK to the punch, and that could help you close that deal.

This is what I can tell you. Five influential people in your business will make you millions of dollars. One good person can help you bring tens of thousands of people to your business. I would trade thousands of followers for one strategic partner that's going to treat this like a business, that has influence, credibility, and is going to run with it with full heart. It's really going to treat it like a business. So, is it worth it? A hundred percent. It's worth it. Will it grow your business so fast? Your head will spin. You'll just be trying to keep up with it. The worst that they can say is no. If you don't call them, they already said no. But if you do call them, it will give you courage to call other people. It will raise your expectations on who you're bringing to the business. You will start to attract other influencers, and they might not be as big and as credible as your first ones, but eventually, you'll attract people way better than they ever were. So do it. Do it now. Do it today, and watch your business explode. Thanks, guys. Make it a great day.

You're not just flipping through another chapter on network marketing; You're stepping into an arena where the timid fear to tread and where the bold reap rewards beyond their wildest dreams. Every giant leap begins with a small step. And in the world of network marketing, we all start from the same spot: Zero. But here's the thing— where you start doesn't determine where you'll end. It's the hustle, the grind, the relentless pursuit of excellence that carves your path from zero to hero. Guess what? If I can do it, so can you.

Coach's Notes: Lance Conrad's narrative illustrates the power of reaching beyond comfort zones. It's an example of the "go big or go home" attitude that defines many success stories in network marketing. The concept of contacting those on your "chicken list" embodies the boldness required in this profession. It's not just about making those new calls; it's about what those calls make of you—a more resilient, ambitious, and fearless entrepreneur.

Through Lance's eyes, we see a strategy unfold: reaching out to influential individuals can exponentially accelerate your business growth. His "good, better, best" challenge lays down a practical roadmap to engaging these key players. It's a call to action for embracing rejection, leveraging mentorship, and harnessing the potential of strategic partnerships.

As someone who personally knows Lance and has witnessed his journey, I can attest to the efficacy of his approach. His courage to reach out, coupled with the strategic mindset of utilizing upline mentors for credibility, sets a blueprint for making significant strides in network marketing.

Remember, the journey to the top is paved with bold moves. Lance's advice isn't just about growth—it's about transformation. It's about how stepping out of your comfort zone and into the realm of possibility can lead to untold success. So, embrace his challenge, step up to the plate, and let your actions today ignite the fuse of your explosive growth tomorrow. The world of network marketing loves boldness, and as Lance shows, boldness coupled with strategic action is an unbeatable combination.

"You can have more than you've got because you can become more than you are. Unless you change who you are, you will always have want you've got."

– Jim Rohn

DORA EDMONSON

- Visionary Founder of an Online Membership Program at Age 62.

- Inspiring Speaker and Consultant with 20+ Years of Experience, while Navigating Motherhood during Spouse's US Navy Service.

- Architect of Profitable Solutions for the Vacation and Real Estate Industries Amidst Economic Challenges.

- Seasoned Trainer and Mentor Specializing in Building Employee and Customer Loyalty.

- Emerging Entrepreneur Thriving in a 40-Year Marriage, Cherished Grandmother to Seven Grandchildren.

Nuture Relationships for a Fulfilling Life

Welcome to the journey of discovering the transformative power of the CARE Strategy. For over four decades, I've navigated life's twists and turns armed with a formula that has fostered stability, reliability, and dependability in my relationships with family, friends, and colleagues online and offline.

As a new consultant, I found myself facing a unique challenge when the CEO approached me, intrigued by the rapid transformation I had instigated within his company. In his four-decade career, he had never witnessed such a swift and dramatic shift in company culture and employee loyalty. My initial response was simple: 'I CARE about them.' However, this seemingly straightforward statement led me to profound reflections. What did it truly mean to care about employees? How did I manage to orchestrate this remarkable turnaround in less than 30 days? How did we elevate our customer service ratings from low to high, and our workplace atmosphere from a negative daily grind to an enthusiastic hub of positivity? It was during these introspective moments that I realized the essence of my approach lay in genuinely demonstrating that I cared about every individual within the organization. From that transformative conversation with the CEO, I crafted the CARE formula—a blueprint not only for cultivating robust, productive teams but also for nurturing profound connections with friends and family.

At the heart of the CARE Strategy lie four pillars that build connections and foster understanding.

Commitment to Consistency: The Steadfast Anchor
Attractive Attention: The Magnetic Force
Realistic Responsibility: The Backbone of Dependability
Engaging with Excellence: Elevating Connections with Sincere Support

In a world where the demands of work and family life often pull us in different directions, finding the balance to nurture relationships can be challenging. This is where the CARE Strategy shines, providing a compass to guide us through the intricacies of life. It's a philosophy rooted in the belief that, while we can't always control life's challenges, we can always control our behavior and attitude in response to them. As you read on, I invite you to reflect on your relationships and consider how the CARE Strategy can bring a new depth and fulfillment to them.

Coach's Notes: Dora introduces the CARE Strategy, a guide for cultivating meaningful connections in both personal and professional realms. This approach centers on Commitment to Consistency, Attractive Attention, Realistic Responsibility, and Engaging with Excellence. Dora's reflections and experiences underline the importance of genuine care in transforming relationships and organizational culture. As you explore the CARE Strategy, consider how its principles can enhance your interactions and deepen bonds with those around you. As always take notes because Dora always has great content!

Commitment to Consistency: The Steadfast Anchor

Now, let's dive into the first pillar of the CARE Strategy: Commitment to Consistency.

Steps to living a Commitment to Consistency

- **Prioritize People**: Focus on people over projects. Do you keep a follow-up list to track commitments?

- **Manage My Reactions**: Do I know what triggers me? Do I have a plan to deal with those triggers?

- **Track My Commitments**: Do I document and regularly review promises I made? Am I tracking what I say I will do, and am I doing it when I said I would?

As a 62-year-old grandma venturing into the world of social media, it was my desire to create real friendships online. Being disabled and homebound, I aimed to develop a support system of friends in the digital realm. I recognized the importance of being consistent and positive in building this community of friends. My goal was to stand out and provide value in my posts and support for others. I wanted to be a dependable source of encouragement and assistance for those in my online circle.

To illustrate the importance of Commitment to Consistency, let me share a personal story. As a leader in a social media business, my team was grappling with maintaining consistency in their daily social media tasks. Recognizing their challenges, I was determined to offer guidance and support. To address this issue, I introduced a daily accountability call where team members could gather to focus on their engagement efforts. Every day, I make it a point to be present on that call, ready to roll up my sleeves and work alongside them. This serves as a powerful reminder that they're not alone in their journey and that they have someone readily available to address any questions or concerns.

The journey toward a commitment to consistency isn't a walk in the park. It demands time, effort, and dedication to put these principles into practice. By implementing this daily accountability call, I aimed to not only emphasize the importance of consistency but also provide a tangible means for my team to cultivate this essential trait in their daily routines. Together, we've embarked on this journey, reinforcing the value of reliability and dependability, both in our professional and personal lives.

As a parent of three young children, I came to understand the profound importance of creating a stable home environment. When I was upset, it wasn't just me affected—it had a ripple effect on my children, often spoiling the day for everyone. I yearned to build a positive and stable haven for my kids, a place where they could rely on stability, encouragement, and love. I wanted our home to be their sanctuary, a place where they could find solace from the challenges of the world outside. I realized that while I couldn't control their experiences beyond our home's walls, I could certainly ensure that home was a haven of consistency and dependability. I wanted my children to know that their mom was a steadfast and reliable presence in their lives.

As parents we were interested in the hobbies of our children. I learned to play online computer games so I could join their Friday night dungeon runs. Yes, I am a proud level 64 warrior in World of Warcraft. I participate in the Family Fantasy Football Leagues and usually take 1st place in the weekly confidence picks. I build worlds with my grandkids in Minecraft and do a pretty good job in Roblox. Believe me it takes time, energy and planning to engage with our children and grandchildren, but it is well worth the memories and opportunities to share life lessons.

Today, my adult children know that they can always turn to me for positivity and support. They cherish memories of laughter and problem-solving. Our home might not have been perfect, but when challenges arose, they learned that we faced them together, consistently moving forward. Consistency, both in attitudes and actions, played a vital role in building the stability and trust that define our family.

Commitment to Consistency isn't just about being there; it's about being a rock-solid presence that others can always count on. Moving on to the next aspect of the CARE Strategy, let's explore Attractive Attention.

Coach's Notes: Diving into the CARE Strategy, the first pillar, Commitment to Consistency, emphasizes the importance of prioritizing people, managing reactions, and tracking commitments. This approach is time tested, not just in professional settings but also in personal settings, like social media and family life. By fostering a consistent presence, whether through daily accountability calls in a business context or engaging with family in meaningful activities, this principle cultivates reliability and trust. As we progress through the CARE Strategy, the focus on Attractive Attention next promises to further enrich our understanding of building and nurturing relationships. Remember successful people just do the basics better.

Attractive Attention: The Magnetic Force

While Commitment to Consistency focuses on reliability, Attractive Attention emphasizes being fully present. It challenges us to put down our phones and genuinely engage with those around us, whether in face-to-face interactions or through the realm of social media.

Steps to living Attractive Attention

- **Learn to Maintain Eye Contact**: Do you listen with your eyes and ears? It is important to give your full attention to the person speaking to you both in conversations online and offline.

- **Practice Hands-Free Interaction**: Keep your hands free from distractions during conversations to remain fully present.

- **Excel in Active Listening**: Listen carefully to individuals and repeat back what you've heard to ensure understanding and clarity.

I'll be the first to admit, I'm inherently an obsessive person. My natural focus and determination are strengths, but they can also be weaknesses. My husband quickly learned that when he enters my office to talk to me, he needs to capture my attention, or his words fall on deaf ears. My eyes must lock onto him, or I won't truly hear what he's saying. Being project-oriented, it was often a challenge for me to shift my focus away from work when my children were young. To overcome this, I learned to compartmentalize my tasks and finish my work during work hours, allowing me to be fully present with my kids without distractions. I discovered that paying attention was the key to nurturing our relationship.

Here's a real-life example that highlights the significance of Attractive Attention in our relationships. My husband is a deliberate communicator. He enjoys sharing jokes and stories at a leisurely pace. Even after forty years of marriage, it still requires considerable patience on my part to allow him the time to finish his conversations or questions before I respond. Paying attention has always been a personal challenge for me as I tend to get absorbed in my own thoughts and the direction I'm headed.

Over time, I've learned to prioritize my husband's words by watching him closely when he speaks, taking a deep breath before responding to provide him the necessary time to finish his statements, and repeating back what he said to ensure that I'm truly hearing and understanding his perspective. These deliberate steps have not only improved our communication but have also deepened our connection over the years. They underscore the essence of 'Attractive Attention'—being fully present and engaged in the conversations that matter most.

I've also found that the same principle applies to social media. When I pay attention to others, I attract them to me. People want to feel valued and that they matter. Building connections online is just as much about paying attention, showing genuine interest, and making friends as it is in the offline world. People are fundamentally the same, whether we interact with them in person or online.

Children will teach you that you must listen and take the time to focus; otherwise, you might miss important signs of their thoughts and actions. Repeating back what I heard and clarifying their wishes has become second nature. It takes practice to truly listen to questions or comments before my mouth jumps to an answer. But in the end, the results are worth the effort. When you pay attention to others and prioritize their messages first, you attract more people and build a stronger community around you.

Attractive Attention is not just about listening; it's about making the other person feel seen and valued, a cornerstone of the CARE Strategy. In contrast to the previous pillar, Realistic Responsibility deals with accountability in a different way.

Realistic Responsibility: The Backbone of Dependability

To recap, we've discussed Commitment to Consistency and Attractive Attention. Now, let's delve into Realistic Responsibility. Realistic Responsibility calls us to take ownership of our actions, leaving no room for excuses or justifications. It's about acknowledging our stumbles, making amends, and being responsible for our commitments, both in the face-to-face world and on social media. Now, think about your own life. How do you manage your responsibilities, and what strategies do you use to stay realistic and accountable?

Steps to Living with Realistic Responsibility

- **Strive to Evaluate Realistically**: Do you regularly assess your ability to meet goals, and align expectations with the time and resources available? It is vital to understand what I can and cannot do.

- **Set Clear Expectations**: When apologizing, do I express my feelings honestly, do I focus on my actions rather than excuses, and have I established realistic priorities?

In life, we wear many hats—spouses, parents, grandparents, friends, and professionals. Each role brings its own set of demands, and the juggling act can often feel overwhelming.

As a mother and an executive, I came to a profound realization: I couldn't control time. We all have the same 24 hours in a day. What I could control, however, was how I managed the demands within that time frame. I adopted a systematic approach, relying on checklists and a love for processes. I broke down my life into manageable steps, taking it one day at a time. My year-long calendar held the big picture: Birthdays, projected vacation days, holidays, and school breaks. The monthly calendar added more detail, including activities and significant events. Then came the weekly calendar, where I delved into specific times for events. Finally, the daily calendar spelled out the nitty-gritty details for each project and commitment. Each night, I reviewed the next day's tasks, ensuring I was prepared.

In today's digital age, I've extended this organization to include a social media calendar. It outlines what posts I need to make on each platform and the type of content I'll share. It even factors in how many engagements I'll aim for each day. This deliberate planning not only keeps me on track but also helps me manage my time on social media effectively. It is easy to get carried away on social media and scroll through for hours instead of minutes. Setting a timer to track my time is beneficial.

I have also learned to take responsibility for the results on social media. Instead of blaming the algorithm for a lack of engagement, I take responsibility. I ask myself, "Have I been engaging with others?" The results are tied directly to my own engagement with others. Do I want results, then who am I engaging with to get results? If I want engagement, the question is, "Am I engaging?" The answer is simple. If I want reactions and comments, then I must be reacting and commenting!

Two valuable lessons became apparent to me along the way. First, understanding my responsibilities and being realistic about when I could fulfill them was essential. Overbooking and trying to be in two places at once were recipes for stress and chaos. Second, most stress stems from setting unrealistic expectations. Scheduling back-to-back appointments with no breaks or expecting to make school pickups within fifteen minutes of a meeting were simply unrealistic. Realistic Responsibility emerged as a vital principle for me, allowing me to maintain peace and stability in my daily life.

Realistic Responsibility is not just about meeting expectations; it's about setting them wisely and owning our journey, a crucial aspect of the CARE Strategy.

Engaging with Excellence: Elevating Connections with Sincere Support

As we've seen in the previous section, Realistic Responsibility plays a crucial role in managing life's demands. Now, let's see how it relates to the fourth pillar, Engaging with Excellence.

Engaging with Excellence extends an invitation to uplift others, to be a reliable and encouraging presence, and to contribute value through our social media connections. Whether it's through offering encouragement, entertainment, education, or empowerment, engaging with excellence has the power to transform ordinary interactions into extraordinary connections. Think of a time when someone's support made a difference in your life. How can you replicate that impact in your interactions with others?

Steps to Engaging with Excellence

- **Cultivate Gratitude**: Reflect daily on reasons to be thankful for others and how they enrich your life.

- **Celebrate Strengths**: Acknowledge and celebrate the positive attributes and strengths of those around you.

- **Share in Victories**: Actively listen to others accomplishments and join in their celebration.

- **Embrace Positivity**: Maintain a positive outlook, focus on solutions, and inspire hope in interactions.

Over time, I honed my communication skills, both in everyday life and online interactions. My social media mentor imparted a crucial concept that I've carried with me: Engage with others by sharing content that either educates, entertains, encourages, or empowers them. If I couldn't engage with excellence in mind, I refrained from sharing a post or starting a conversation. This principle has been instrumental in building my communication skills and fostering meaningful connections.

As my children have grown older, I've found that I have less advice to give them. I've learned to wait for them to ask for my opinion and to share what they need to hear rather than what I want to say. Their best interests aren't always the same as my opinions. As a grandparent, it can be challenging to resist the urge to lecture my adult children on parenting my grandchildren.

However, I've come to realize that they love their children just as much as I do, and they want what's best for them. I've learned to share stories instead of opinions, to believe in them, and to encourage them in their parenting journey.

Engaging with Excellence is a timeless principle that continues to guide me today as a parent, grandparent, wife, and friend. It's a skill set that I practice daily. Engaging with Excellence is not just a practice but a lifestyle, embodying the core values of the CARE Strategy in every interaction. Now that we've explored the four pillars individually, it's time to understand how they come together to form the complete CARE Strategy.

Nurturing Stability through CARE

With a solid understanding of each pillar, we're ready to conclude our journey through the CARE Strategy. Life, with all its demands, calls us to a simple yet profound answer: Care about others' needs first. Putting the CARE Strategy into practice may not be easy. It will require a daily commitment to learn these skills, but the results will pay off tenfold.

Steps to Embracing the CARE Strategy:

- **Practice Self-Compassion**: Recognize that personal growth takes time. Reflect on your progress weekly, acknowledging both growth and areas for improvement.

- **Prioritize Honestly:** List your daily tasks and relationships in order of importance, focusing on the top priorities each day.
- **Choose a Focus Area:** Start by concentrating on one specific area or relationship where the CARE Strategy can be applied.
- **Build Habits Gradually:** Develop positive habits step by step, focusing on consistency for long-term change.

Throughout our exploration of the CARE Strategy, we've uncovered the transformative power of Commitment to Consistency, Attractive Attention, Realistic Responsibility, and Engaging with Excellence. This strategy isn't just about improving how we interact with others; it's about enriching our lives with connections that are rooted in understanding, respect, and genuine care.

As we wrap up our exploration of the CARE Strategy, consider how these principles can enhance your relationships and interactions. As Jordan Peterson reminds us, we all have untapped potential. Embracing the CARE Strategy is a step towards realizing that potential in our relationships.

> *"You are more than you are today.*
> *You are more than you think you can be."*
>
> *— Jordan Peterson*

Coach's Notes: Dora shares insights into living with Realistic Responsibility, focusing on evaluating abilities, setting clear expectations, and managing life's multiple roles effectively. Her journey, from a social media novice to a seasoned professional, underscores the importance of commitment and realistic goal-setting in fostering genuine online and offline connections.

Dora's strategic use of calendars for planning and her disciplined approach to social media engagement highlight her methodical method to life's challenges. She emphasizes taking responsibility for outcomes rather than blaming external factors, encouraging proactive engagement for desired results.

Her personal stories, from adjusting her parenting approach to engaging with her children and grandchildren's interests, reflect a deep understanding of meaningful interactions. Dora's experiences remind us of the power of realistic assessment and the impact of positivity and consistency in relationship building.

My mantra is:

"Create bonds with your dreams,

and let yourself rise and believe."

ALEJANDRA ARAGONÉS

- Science education background with a strong passion for dancing.
- Owned a dance studio for 10 years. It lead me to enter the health and wellness world.
- Health, Mindfulness and Hemp CBD Coach since 2018.
- Network marketer since 2020.
- Mom of two beautiful souls that are my everyday inspiration to make a difference in this world.

Embracing Transformation:
From Brick-and-Mortar to Online Success

I've always thought that doing what you love and finding joy in it is the secret sauce for feeling happy every day. But what if that thing you're passionate about starts to stress you out? Do you keep pushing through, or is there a way to change things up?

I've always believed that following your passions and finding genuine happiness are super important for feeling good day-to-day. But life can throw curveballs, and something you used to love can turn into a total headache.

When you hit those rough patches, it's tempting to just keep pushing forward. We're kinda programmed to never give up, right? But in the middle of all that chaos, there's a chance for something big. It's like a moment where you can stop and really think about what's going on, and maybe make some changes. So, do you stay stuck in feeling miserable, or do you gather up the guts to try something totally new?

Looking back on my younger years, I always knew what I wanted. I wanted to be a teacher and I loved dancing more than anything. Since I was nine, I dreamed of having my own dance studio, and eventually, that dream came true. But then, a bunch of foot injuries messed up my plans of becoming a pro dancer. Still, I promised myself that dancing would always be a big part of my life.

Alongside dancing, I was also into math and physics, which led me to become a Physics Engineer. I got into Econophysics and thought I'd end up in finance. But during job interviews, all they seemed to care about was when we'd finish work. I decided I wasn't going to give up my dancing or teaching dreams for some boring corporate job.

Then, everything changed. I got this amazing chance to start my own dance studio. I was only twenty three and about to make my lifelong dream come true. The idea of having a place where people could come and dance with passion and purpose got me super excited. Over the next ten years, my studio became a hub of awesome experiences, teaching me so much along the way. It showed me how much I loved helping others and fueled my passion for teaching, as I guided young dancers to be strong and confident.

In that studio, dancing was more than just moving around; it was like therapy, a safe space filled with love. But even with all that happiness, I started feeling a shift in my career path.

Through my own journey and the questions my students brought to me, I realized something: Traditional nutrition studies didn't vibe with what I believed in. I didn't want to be all about strict diets and counting calories. Instead, I wanted to focus on nourishing every part of life—nutrition, sure, but also doing things we love, building real connections, and more. So, I decided to switch gears and become a health coach, diving into mindfulness, hemp CBD, and this cool thing called neurodance, which mixes neuroscience and dance. My goal was simple but important: Create a space where students could take care of their health in a way that sticks.

On a personal note, being a mom was always a big deal to me. I promised myself that whatever I did, it had to let me be there for my kid. When I finally became a mom, it just fit into my life perfectly. I loved bringing my little boy with me, whether it was to the dance studio or anywhere else, seeing him happy in every moment. But even with all that joy, there was this nagging question: What do you do when something you love starts feeling like a chore, stealing your happiness?

It was confusing to feel both fulfilled and frustrated. The thing I'd wanted so badly was suddenly weighing me down. The endless nights waiting for late teachers or comforting upset parents were wearing me out. I wasn't just a dance teacher anymore; I was like an unofficial therapist, dealing with people's personal stuff instead of just teaching dance moves.

During my second pregnancy, I started feeling really uneasy. I was all over the place emotionally, sometimes loving my dance studio, other times hating it. Even though I had someone helping out, I felt like I needed more support. Plus, now that my older son was in school, staying up late to deal with studio stuff just wasn't doable anymore. It was frustrating because I wanted to do coaching too, but the studio took up all my time. My husband kept saying I needed to find a balance, which was always important to me.

Then, the pandemic hit, making everything even harder. I was trying to keep the studio going while supporting students and teachers, but it was tough. Money was tight, especially when my assistant left suddenly. Then I had to figure out how to move classes online while recovering from a C-section. It was a lot to deal with, especially since in Mexico, the arts aren't always a top priority.

Coach's Notes: Alejandra Aragonés' journey exemplifies the resilience required to embrace change and thrive amidst life's trials. Transitioning from a passionate dance studio owner to an innovative online success story, Alejandra demonstrates that sometimes, letting go of what we've always known opens the door to new, fulfilling opportunities.

Faced with personal and professional challenges, including health issues and the global pandemic, Alejandra chose to pivot rather than persist in discomfort. This decision wasn't about giving up; it was about adapting to change and redefining success on her own terms. Her story teaches us that boldness in the face of adversity can lead to transformative growth.

Alejandra's approach to integrating her passions with her professional life, especially her focus on holistic health and well-being, highlights the importance of aligning our careers with our core values. It reminds us that true fulfillment comes from pursuing what genuinely makes us happy, even if it means stepping into the unknown.

Her narrative is a testament to the idea that when something we love becomes a source of stress, it's an invitation to reassess and potentially chart a new course. Alejandra's success in navigating this transition serves as inspiration for anyone facing similar crossroads, showing that with courage and resilience, it's possible to turn trials into triumphs. Her story should empower you that anything is possible.

When the second wave of the pandemic hit in January 2021, I knew I had to prioritize safety above everything else. Switching to online classes wasn't just a business decision; it was the right thing to do to protect everyone's health.

But through all this chaos, I started realizing that I couldn't keep sacrificing time with my family for a dream that was fading away. The constant frustration was taking away all the joy I used to find in my work. So, I made the tough call to say goodbye to the studio and embrace the idea of letting go. It took three long months to finally close things down, but in the end, it brought me some much-needed clarity. By letting go of one dream, I made room for new opportunities to come my way. It just goes to show how life can surprise you when you least expect it.

Amidst all the chaos on December 29, 2020, something unexpected popped up—an offer to get involved in network marketing for hemp CBD. I was feeling really stressed out and anxious, especially with a family history of depression. The idea of finding wellness through CBD sounded really appealing, especially since I was already focused on coaching for stress management, which felt kinda ironic given my own struggles at the time.

Deciding to join this venture was a big deal for me—it was like taking a leap of faith into something totally new. Getting the company started in the Mexican market made things even more complicated, but it also taught me a big lesson: You've got to embrace change, face your fears, and be open to transforming yourself. Because in those uncertain moments, there's always a chance for something great to happen. Ever since January 2021, my journey of growing and changing has been pretty amazing.

The title of this part of my life, *Embracing Transformation: From Brick-and-Mortar to Online Success*, really sums up how much things changed. Running a physical store takes up a ton of time, money, and personal sacrifices. Vacations became a thing of the past because I was always tied to the studio's schedule. Even though I tried to be a good boss, I felt like I had to be there all the time, which was exhausting and made me miss out on a lot of life.

Moving my business online, doing coaching and network marketing, was like a breath of fresh air. At first, it was weird not having the studio hustle, but I learned to enjoy having more time for my kids—a real blessing. Every day, I got better at working smarter, figuring out this whole entrepreneurship thing with more clarity.

This journey has been all about me growing personally, and I couldn't have done it without the amazing support from my network. Sure, there are times when I doubt myself, but having people there to help me out keeps me going. It's definitely not an easy journey—it's full of challenges and unexpected turns. But for those brave enough to dive in, it's also full of endless opportunities to explore and find fulfillment. When life gets tough, that's when we really find out what we're made of. Even though tomorrow's uncertain, there's always the promise of growing, changing, and finding happiness along the way.

Taking on entrepreneurship in a more all-around way, I've started to see how everything—my mind, body, and spirit—are all connected. Sure, making money is important, but what I really want is to live a life that feels meaningful and true to myself. This change in how I see things hasn't just affected my business—it's changed everything about how I live.

In the world of network marketing, I've found a group of people who all want the same thing: To feel empowered and have plenty to go around. Working with them has opened my eyes to new ideas and ways of thinking. We support each other and learn from each other, showing that success isn't something you do alone—it's something you do together.

But even with all this excitement and freedom, I make sure to take care of myself. Making sure I'm healthy—physically, emotionally, and spiritually—is my number one priority. Whether it's doing mindfulness exercises or sticking to my workout routine, I've found habits that make me feel good inside and out. I've realized that true success isn't just about getting awards or recognition—it's about feeling peaceful and happy inside.

Coach's Notes: Alejandra Aragonés' story is a profound reminder that embracing change is not just necessary; it's fundamental to thriving in both life and business. My advice? Never shy away from reassessing your path, especially when faced with obstacles that challenge your passion. It's in these moments of uncertainty that the greatest opportunities for growth and transformation lie. Consider every trial as a stepping stone towards a more aligned and fulfilling journey. The courage to pivot and adapt, much like Alejandra did, is what separates those who find deep, meaningful success from those who merely exist in comfort zones.

Moreover, the essence of true success transcends the confines of financial achievements or professional milestones. It's about creating a life rich in joy, health, and purpose. Alejandra's shift towards a more holistic approach to success, balancing entrepreneurship with self-care and community support, underscores the importance of nurturing all facets of your being. My advice to you: Prioritize your well-being as fiercely as you do your business goals. Cultivate a support network that champions collective growth and embraces the journey together. Remember, the path to lasting success is paved with self-care, adaptability, and a community that lifts each other up.

Is it worth it, doing both the online health coaching and network marketing gig? Absolutely. Celebrating my tenth year in the game made it clear. I treated myself to an awesome vacation in Croatia and Italy—something I never would've thought possible before. While I was there, I saw how my work and relaxation could blend seamlessly together, showing me the kind of life I've always wanted. It's not about constantly hustling like society says we should—it's about living authentically and enjoying the simple things, like spending time with family.

The main message of this chapter really hits home—it's all about being okay with change and going after what you love with everything you've got. Life's always changing, and that's just how it goes. It shows how important it is to be flexible and come up with new ideas, especially in an ever-changing industry. Being able to adapt and think outside the box isn't just nice—it's key to making it big.

As we go through life's ups and downs, it's important to keep our eyes open for new opportunities, even if they're not what we had in mind at first. Being open to trying new things, like getting into network marketing, can lead to some pretty amazing growth, both personally and professionally.

A big part of this story is about making sure we're taking care of ourselves first and foremost. Sometimes, that means walking away from stuff that's not making us happy or doesn't line up with our values. It might seem scary to leave behind a regular job, but it's worth it if it means finding a better, more balanced life doing something else.

Don't forget to keep an open mind to new possibilities. Some of the best things in life come from unexpected places, and we've gotta be ready to roll with the punches and grow when those chances come our way. By staying tuned in to what's going on around us and trusting our gut feelings, we set ourselves up for some real personal growth.

Coach's Notes: *Embracing transformation in both life and business is crucial. It's easy to get comfortable, but real growth happens when you're willing to reassess and make changes, especially in the face of adversity. Every challenge is an opportunity to learn and adapt, moving you closer to a more fulfilling journey. My advice? Be bold in your decisions. If something isn't serving you or your happiness anymore, have the courage to pivot. It's not about abandoning your dreams, but rather refining them to align with your evolving self.*

Success isn't solely measured by financial gain or accolades; it's deeply rooted in finding joy, health, and purpose in what you do. Thus, integrating self-care into your daily routine is as important as any business strategy. Surround yourself with a community that supports growth and faces challenges together. By prioritizing well-being and valuing collective success, you cultivate an environment where everyone thrives. Remember, the strongest foundations for success are built on adaptability, wellness, and a supportive network.

At its heart, this story is a call to live life to the fullest, appreciating every moment and going after what makes us happy. Whether it's chasing our dreams, saying "yes" to new opportunities, or just being there for others, it's all about making the most of what we've got. When we take care of ourselves and spread some positive vibes, we make the world a better place for everyone.

Above all, what I hope for isn't just confined to these words—it's a heartfelt invitation for each reader to start their own journey towards happiness, health, and feeling whole. I wish for every breath they take to be filled with joy, blending perfectly with life's natural rhythm. With each step they take, I hope they feel a deep sense of purpose, guiding them towards their dreams and goals. In everything they do, I hope they find fulfillment, igniting their passion and lighting the way to their ultimate destiny.

In this quest for happiness, health, and feeling whole, network marketing stands out as a powerful tool for change. It's not just about making money—it's about personal growth, connecting with others, and feeling empowered. Through this kind of business, people can build resilience, learn new things, and make meaningful connections. Plus, working together in network marketing creates a sense of community and support, helping everyone reach their full potential and make a positive impact. So, as we set out on this journey towards fulfillment, let's embrace what network marketing has to offer and use it to create lives full of abundance, purpose, and happiness.

As I navigate the ups and downs of online entrepreneurship, I'm reminded every day of how important it is to be adaptable and resilient. Things are always changing, so being able to roll with the punches and come up with new ideas is crucial. Embracing change like this has helped me tackle challenges and grab hold of opportunities with strength and grace. It's all about staying positive and believing that every obstacle is just a chance to grow and transform.

Looking ahead, I'm feeling pretty pumped up and excited. Every day brings chances to learn, grow, and try new things. Whether it's expanding my business, deepening my friendships, or diving into new interests, I'm all in for living a life that feels meaningful and true. And as I keep figuring things out about myself, I'm reminded that we've all got the power to make our dreams happen.

To wrap it up, I'm sending out some good vibes to anyone out there starting their own journey of change. I hope you find the guts to embrace whatever comes your way, the strength to push through tough times, and the smarts to follow your heart. May your path be lit up with possibilities, and may you always remember how awesome you really are. Here's to making big changes, grabbing onto opportunities, and living a life that's full of purpose, excitement, and happiness.